A Mother's Tears

Poems of Heartbreak, Loss, and Discovery

To our precious son, Graham.
Your light will shine forever.

March 30, 1985 – September 22, 2007

CONTENTS

ACKNOWLEDGEMENTS

Throughout the many changes in my life my mother has been the one constant I could always rely upon. Her unending love and support have helped guide me through all the difficult times in my life. I treasure our relationship. What a blessing it is to have a loving mother as well as dearest friend. Thank you mother, for your wisdom, patience, and grace. I am so grateful to be your daughter. Some angels live among us – thank you for being one of mine. I love you more than words can say.

A heartfelt thank you also to the friends who have reached out and been here for me during the most devastating time of my life. Your compassion and caring gave me hope when it felt as if all hope were gone. You continue to be beacons of light.

To my husband and Graham's loving father, Sam, with deep appreciation for your beautiful photographs and support in the creation of this special book. We honor our beloved son and the love we continue to share with him.

INTRODUCTION

For as long as I can remember, I wanted to be a mother. My dream came true when I married and was blessed with the birth of two wonderful children. I found such joy in being the mother of a beautiful daughter, Laura, and a terrific son, Graham. They gave so much purpose and meaning to my life. I dedicated myself to my family and their well-being.

In September 2007 my son had just started his senior year in college. We were all excited about his final year and anticipating his graduation and career plans. As a gifted graphic design major, Graham had many ideas about what he wanted to do. There was such satisfaction in seeing him happy and growing in confidence and maturity, making plans for his future. It is what every mother wants for her children.

In a few seconds, that all disappeared. Graham loved to walk. After being out late one night with some friends he decided to walk back to his apartment. It was a beautiful night. There was a lovely full moon and the stars were bright. Graham was talking with his good friend on his cell phone for part of his walk. His friend later told us that Graham was very happy. They were discussing ideas about their senior portfolio. Graham was also talking about plans for a date he had made with a young lady he was interested in for the next day. Shortly after that phone call, as he continued walking, Graham somehow fell to his death from the highway bridge he was walking across.

The shock and trauma of my son's death cast me into a world I no longer knew. Losing a child is a form of hell. There is no other word to describe the pain. I couldn't stand the separation. Graham's death catapulted me into a desperate search for meaning. I felt like so much of my purpose in life was gone. I turned inward, searching for understanding and continued connection. Meditating every morning became a necessity. I would pray for acceptance and peace as the tears ran down my face. The greatest longing of my soul was to feel that he was still with me. I also yearned to make sense out of what appeared to be so totally senseless. I believe that I am slowly gaining insight as I travel this agonizing journey of grief.

Around Valentine's Day of 2009, seventeen months after my son's death, the words "only son, treasured one" kept going through my mind.

I didn't want to forget them, so I went to write them down, and kept on writing. I thought that I was journaling. It wasn't until I stopped writing and read what I had written that I realized it was a poem. I had never written a poem before. Since that day I have written a continuous stream of poems. They are an affirmation that spirit and love are eternal. I am so grateful for this amazing unfoldment.

The poems have been helping me put my broken pieces back together. I felt I should share them through this book. It is my dearest wish that these poems may help other broken-hearted people, because out of the greatest darkness and tragedy there can also be hope and healing and light. Love and blessings to all who are on this walk.

Love Never Ends

Rainbow Bridge

I'm going to meet you halfway, Graham, come take my hand,
I'm walking steadily toward the Promised Land,
I won't let you leave me, I'm not far behind,
You are with me always, son of mine.

One foot in Heaven, and one foot on Earth,
I straddle both worlds now, a totally new turf,
Like a rainbow's promise on a distant ridge,
Let us join together and make a bridge.

My Precious Son

❧

Every child born into the world is a new thought of God, an ever fresh and radiant possibility.

Kate Douglas Wiggin

Only Son

Only son, treasured one,
How swiftly time has flown,
Such a handsome man you had grown,
Promise born, from my arms you were torn,
Broken heart, shattered dreams,
Can this be as it seems?

Daily tears, how many years can one weep?
Let me sleep and not awake,
For surely this was some dread mistake,
Lost, confused, where to turn?
For connection is what I yearn.

Purpose was, but what purpose is,
When so much focus was his?
Each day I try to walk and try to talk,
Searching for what was lost.

Daily prayers for hope reborn.
Will I always be forlorn?
Precious memories, let grief abate,
And help me to celebrate,
That which was and still endures,
Love, the blessed cure.

This was my first poem.

A Big Bouquet of Balloons

If I could be one of the balloons,
Released to our children gone too soon,
I would joyously sail straight to you,
Among the clouds in a sky of blue.

Without a care,
And light as air,
My sorrow would slip away,
Leaving behind unhappy days.

A loving mother with her dearest son,
Together once again,
What a dream this would be,
If it were a possibility.

As the balloons float to you above,
I know you feel all my love,
Sent to you with joy and tears,
For every single precious year.

You filled my heart for all time,
I am so grateful you were mine,
Watch for me, I'll join you soon,
With a big bouquet of beautiful balloons.

A Greater Story

Who would know that you would fall,
To be taken from us all,
You had much more life to live,
Artistic talent to create and give.

You wanted to be the best,
And you stood out from the rest,
Single-mindedly you pursued,
All the ideas that came to you.

Dedicated, a visionary, an artist,
You always worked your hardest,
To share the pictures in your mind,
With the rest of mankind.

Maybe here your work was done,
The plan must be a bigger one,
And on greater tides of glory,
You continue to write your story.

Weave your magic once again,
With your messages from Heaven,
Reminding us every day,
Of the love you send our way.

Though your body died,
You are still alive,
Helping us to see,
Glimpses of eternity.

A Missing Piece

Blindsided, torn apart,
With a fractured, broken heart,
What am I here for?
My life is strewn across the floor,
Like a jigsaw puzzle with a missing piece,
Will I ever be at ease,
With the anguish inside of me,
For the picture that will never be?

The old picture that was you,
Was what I wanted, not something new,
I love you more than I can say,
And every day you've been away,
Leaves a big empty space,
That nothing can ever replace,
Help me build my life anew,
Make it possible for me to do.

With God's help and all your love,
Show me what I am capable of,
That a new picture, while not the old,
Can still be worthwhile for me to hold,
Although your body died,
I feel you always by my side,
The memory of our time together,
Will live with me forever.

A Moment in Time

The last thing you did before you drove away,
On a beautiful September day,
To help out your dad and me,
Was plant a lovely crape myrtle tree.

It was the last one planted out of five,
To be enjoyed while we're on the patio outside,
I watched you while you were hard at work,
Digging up all that dirt.

"Let me take your picture," I said,
And you smiled and turned your head,
I took a wonderful picture of you,
Beside the crape myrtle when you were through.

The following weekend you were dead,
There are no words that can be said,
You were here one moment, the next you were gone,
And we are left to struggle on.

Who could know that picture would be our last,
Of the twenty-two years that had passed,
From our darling baby to handsome young man,
We are working hard to understand.

I treasure that picture that now hangs on our wall,
A special moment in time to recall,
And when I look at the crape myrtle tree,
I see your beloved face smiling at me.

A Shooting Star

You were like starlight,
Burning bright,
Vibrating with intensity,
With all that you came here to be.

Like a shooting star in the sky,
Glorious, but quickly passing by,
How could we know your life would be so fleeting,
Leaving us to search for meaning?

The duality of living here,
Is often filled with fear,
I want the oneness that is true,
To still be able to connect with you.

Concepts that might not resonate with some,
But a journey I have consciously begun,
Following the trail you blazed for me,
Take my hand and help me to see.

As I strive with all my might,
To get beyond this dark night,
Because love can never disappear,
You will always be right here.

A Time to Die

I wish that I could have said goodbye,
Before you died,
Sometimes I imagine you as you fell,
A kind of hell.

I cannot go there,
Without deep despair,
I force my mind to turn away,
To focus on all our other days.

You were happy walking,
On your cell phone talking,
To a good friend,
Shortly before your end.

You were sharing ideas about your art,
What you would start,
Plans, projects, your senior portfolio,
Which direction you would go.

Your last college year,
You were in high gear,
Full of ideas and dreams,
That you wanted to be seen.

If there is a time to die,
I am grateful that you passed on a high,
At the top of your game,
With no one to blame.

To know you were laughing and full of light,
Enjoying your walk on a beautiful night,
Helps me to know,
It was a positive way for you to go.

No pain, no disease,
In seconds you were free,
I can imagine your surprise,
When you realized you had died.

We are all now on a different walk,
Not ever consciously sought,
But maybe part of a bigger plan,
We don't yet fully understand.

We suffer and we grieve,
But I believe,
That eventually we will see,
What we came here to do and be.

Earthly Eyes Cannot See

Earthly eyes cannot see,
That you walk next to me,
Hand in hand by my side,
With me always as I stride.

On earth you were my treasured son,
In Heaven still linked with me as one,
Heartbreaking to not have you here,
But your spirit is always near.

I am working as hard as I can,
To understand the Master plan,
Turn this lead into gold,
Transformation for my soul.

You were not mine to keep,
Love, the blessing for us to reap,
I am so grateful to have been your mother,
And for every moment with each other.

The bonds of love are eternal,
Forming a perfect circle,
Whether in your dimension or mine,
Forever intertwined.

Graham

Our son, you will be forever young,
A handsome man with a heart of gold,
Never having to grow old,
Eternally twenty-two,
To all who knew you.

A loving son and remarkable young man,
Even within your short life span,
You had an amazing mind and tremendous drive,
The power to succeed and thrive,
A visionary artist with a great sense of style,
And the most beautiful smile.

For every wonderful year that we had,
In the joy of being your mom and dad,
For all the love that we knew,
We honor and thank you.

Grains of Sand

I watched you suffer, and I suffered too,
Growing up was so hard for you,
A vulnerable, sensitive boy,
Life was difficult for you to enjoy.

I did my very best,
To help you find happiness,
You worked hard and were doing well,
So many ideas for you to tell.

I admired your determination,
Your strength of will and dedication,
You persevered and made great strides,
Fighting against life's tides.

I thought that as your mother,
We would always be together,
Loving and encouraging you,
In everything you wanted to do.

An upside-down world for you to die before me,
Six months shy of twenty-three,
Just when you were about to go out on your own,
To realize the seeds you'd sown.

You were only passing through,
Twenty-two years was all we knew,
Like little grains of sand,
Time slid through my hand.

I cannot yet fully grasp,
What from me has been asked,
How do I let you go,
When you are part of my very soul?

I search for strength from my inner core,
To be happy and filled with joy once more,
Because the love that ran so deep,
Is forever ours to keep.

Hard to be True

I still find it hard to be true,
That it's been nineteen months since I last saw you,
Every day I still cry,
Wondering why you had to die.

I just want you to come home,
Without you I feel so alone,
My whole world is upside down,
I never imagined you'd not be around.

How do we get beyond physical death?
It steals our very breath,
I want to progress spiritually,
But still long to have you here with me.

Sometimes life feels like a maze,
And I wander in a daze,
Searching for inner meaning,
A plan and purpose worth believing.

Awareness on a higher plane,
Is what I want to attain,
Answers as to why I'm here,
And why the cost is so dear.

So that I may learn,
For what I yearn,
Gifts from Spirit that help bring,
Connection, love, and understanding.

Heart Song

The haunting strains,
Of love's sweet refrain,
Softly play,
Throughout my days.

Beautiful notes of memories past,
Music that will forever last,
Up and down the distant chords,
Remind me of times adored.

No matter the tune that I now hear,
In the background your song is clear,
Gently fingering my heartstrings,
Songs of love and remembering.

Beautiful melodies intertwining,
With love and joy realigning,
Two hearts that beat as one,
In harmony with my beloved son.

I See You

I see you when I close my eyes,
Or with my eyes open wide,
Whether I am awake or asleep,
When I laugh or when I weep.

I see you in a baby's smile,
And in the laughter of a child,
When watching boys play and run,
With sticks and toys having fun.

I see you in my dreams at night,
And with the early morning light,
In a lovely pale blue sky,
Watching clouds floating by.

I see you in the twinkling stars,
Gazing upward from afar,
When I look at your apple trees,
And in the gentle morning breeze.

I see you in every change of season,
Or for no specific reason,
In a song that will play,
You are with me every day.

I see you in funny stories,
Crazy movies and artistic glory,
When visiting with your friends,
Everything reminds me of you again.

I see you with all the love I have to give,
Your body died but you still live,
My dearest son and dream come true,
I see you.

If I Could

If I could, I would hold you tight,
I would hug you with all my might,
I would never let you go,
My son, I love you so.

I never wanted to say goodbye,
Every day I still cry,
Why can't you be here?
It's so lonely without you near.

You filled my life with so much joy,
But now there is a terrible void,
What can ever fill the hole,
That has been torn into my very soul?

The anguish is almost more than I can stand,
What is my life's plan?
I thought I was doing what I came here to do,
There was so much meaning in being the mother of you.

I pray for Spirit to enter in,
To feel God's love from within,
And with divine wisdom come to see,
What my soul's purpose is now to be.

If Only

If only dreams could come true,
I would still be with you,
We would never count the days,
Because you would not have passed away.

Each morning when I rise,
There would be no thought that you died,
Every day I would awake with joy,
Happy with life and my wonderful boy.

Sometimes dreams come to an end,
I'll not see my son in this life again,
He's the last thought when I go to bed at night,
And my first thought with the morning light.

If only you were not really dead,
And would be coming home instead,
I'd like to pretend you've just been away for a while,
Separated by nothing more than miles.

Time moves differently now that you are gone,
It's so hard to keep moving on,
You are remembered and loved more than I can say,
And I miss you every single day.

If Only I Could See You

You are now a shining light,
Having walked through Heaven's door,
Reassuring us you're happy,
Returning to spirit form once more.

I know my time is not done here,
And you cannot come home,
If I could just visit you each day,
I'd not feel so alone.

If I could climb God's stairway,
I know where I would be,
Spending time with you again,
So contentedly.

I miss your physical presence,
Your handsome, precious face,
I want to hug and kiss you,
And feel your warm embrace.

There are a million I love yous,
That I would like to say,
Along with all the thank yous,
For every shared day.

I miss you more than ever,
Although you're eternally in my heart,
If only I could see you,
It would ease my broken heart.

I'll Love You Forever

Please give me a message, show me a sign,
Let me know we're connected through time,
Physically parted, souls still entwined,
I'll love you forever, child of mine.

You were once a part of me,
My cherished little baby,
A treasured son come to earth,
When I was blessed to give you birth.

I sang you sweet lullabies,
Quieted your baby cries,
I soothed your childhood fears,
Dried away all your tears.

You filled my life in so many ways,
Bringing purpose to my days,
I couldn't have loved you any more than I do,
How can your life be through?

Where are you now my son?
I'll miss you forever precious one,
Our years together seem like a dream,
What does my life now mean?

My world has been torn apart,
But you are written across my heart,
You will always be a part of me,
Connected through eternity.

Light of Love

I light a candle for you each night,
And watch the flame burning bright,
A visual remembrance of the love we knew,
When we were blessed to have you.

The golden glow its warmth imparts,
And keeps you within my heart,
Surrounded by you night and day,
Forever you will stay,
Within my thoughts, my heart, my mind,
Through all the passages of time.

Love Never Ends

Do you remember when,
You'd speculate about life's end,
Not sure if the soul went on,
When the body was gone?

Ironic, now to me,
When you are no longer on the earth to see,
All the signs that you give,
To let us know the soul still lives.

Thank you for the proof you're sharing,
For all your love and caring,
To help us in our despair,
To become more spiritually aware.

Although in a different dimension,
We can still have connection,
It's not the way I want it to be,
I wish you were here physically.

But I am working hard each day,
To accept my life in this different way,
As I walk this lonely road,
You help relieve my heavy load.

You give me strength so that I can see,
Your love and Heaven's guiding me,
Repairing my heart so that I may mend,
By showing me that love never ends.

My Darling Little Boy

When you were my darling little boy,
I would sing you children's songs with joy,
Lying beside you on your bed,
My precious little sleepy head.

I would sing your favorite songs,
Some were short and some were long,
You would listen happily,
Curled up cozily next to me.

A special time for us to share,
You and me and your teddy bear,
With your baby blanket clutched to your face,
I would snuggle you in a warm embrace.

With your head upon your pillow,
I sang, "How Much Is That Doggie In the Window,"
And the song, "My Grandfather's Clock,"
With the rhythmic words, tick tock, tick tock.

I would kiss you on your little cheeks,
And tell you, now you go to sleep,
Tucking you in for the night,
I would then turn off your light.

Your death cannot take away,
These memories of our precious days,
Moments that live forever,
Within my heart to treasure.

I love you.

My Heart Keeps Beating

Somehow my heart keeps beating,
And I am still breathing,
The sun rises each morning and sets each night,
Evening darkness and morning light.

The world still revolves and life moves on,
But it's fundamentally altered now that you are gone,
I miss you son, I miss my friend,
I never imagined your life would end.

Two years ago you passed away,
But it feels like only yesterday,
I sometimes imagine that you'll walk through our door,
Coming home to visit once more.

I would give anything for this to be true,
To have the life back that we knew,
Mentally I know there's a purpose for this to be,
Emotionally I just want you here with me.

You live in my heart every minute of every day,
Feel the love I send your way,
Thank you Graham, for being my son,
My heart's joy and treasured one.

My Precious Boy

My precious boy,
Great source of joy,
In you I thought I had forever,
I never imagined our tie could sever.

Life is not always what it seems,
Help me, God, to understand what this means,
Why would death take you away?
I thought you'd be here for all my days.

Your life was so fleeting, it went by too fast,
But the treasured memories will always last,
I pray I learn to let go of this sorrow,
It hurts too much to think of tomorrow.

Mystery

Several weeks before you died,
We were sitting on the sofa, side by side,
You looked at me and sort of jokingly said,
"You know, mom, I'm a genius."

You often claimed to be a genius in a light-hearted way,
It was an amusing thing that you would say,
We laughed and we smiled,
And I replied, "That could be,
Thinking that you had always been remarkable to me.

You next said, as an aside,
That geniuses often don't live very long lives,
I acknowledged that this was true,
But didn't make any connection with you.

You were not ill at ease,
It was just an observation made to me,
I wish that I had asked you then,
If you had some premonition.

But when your son is healthy and alive,
You don't consider that he might die,
Could it be that your soul knew,
The transition you would shortly be going through?

There are many mysteries that the universe holds,
And I long to have answers told,
I pray for divine wisdom and insight,
So I may surrender into the light,
And be at peace with life's questions,
As I journey towards you and Heaven.

Never Forgotten

Although your earthly time is done,
You will never be forgotten, my son,
I will love you forever,
And honor and remember.

As long as I live, you will live too,
You are part of all I do,
You share my heartbeats, share my breath,
What is this thing called death?

When I shed my body, I will gladly fly,
To that glorious kingdom in the sky,
Knowing you are waiting for me,
Brings me a sense of serenity.

I will do my best with my remaining years,
Working through my pain and tears,
To rediscover inner peace and joy,
Until we're reunited, my precious boy.

No Crybabies

I often see the Pro-Trucks store,
With the graphic you designed on their door,
The graphic that reads,
"No Crybabies."

I was thinking,
As I was weeping,
That I must be strong,
But this road is long.

With many downs and ups,
I feel as if I am on the cusp,
Of a different direction,
A course correction.

Is your graphic a message for me,
A reminder of what not to be?
I want to laugh and to smile,
Knowing every moment we shared was worthwhile.

That no matter the length of time,
I was blessed to call you mine,
I'll remember and cherish,
Because our love will never perish.

Shining Star

Wherever I am, there you are,
My bright and shining golden star,
A beacon of love helping me,
Become all I am meant to be.

The physical body dies,
But the soul survives,
And with your eternal support and love,
You guide me to what I am capable of.

Broken open from pain and loss,
On my knees with the cost,
I pray the scars on my heart will mend,
Knowing that love never ends.

Sweetest Baby

Sweetest baby, precious boy,
You brought us so much joy,
You were busy from day one,
Keeping me on the run.

You were always in a hurry,
Giving me times of worry,
You crawled, you walked much too fast,
I hoped that my energy would last.

Baby, toddler, little boy,
All the stages to enjoy,
Teenage guy to bright young man,
What an adventurous life span.

Grateful for the gift of you,
We think of you in all we do,
Thanking God for the time we had,
Praying we'll not always be so sad.

The Blink of an Eye

Twenty-two years went by,
In the blink of an eye,
One moment, a newborn in my arms,
And the next, a young man, gone.

Why was it you that died and not me?
This is not how it's supposed to be,
I would gladly take your place,
If we could change time's face.

I gave you life so that you could live,
I gave you all that I could give,
Then you suddenly disappeared,
And somehow I am still here.

So many dreams we'll never know,
No more years to watch you grow,
Only memories for us to keep,
For a life that was far too brief.

The Hands of Time

If I could turn back the hands of time,
You would still be a child of mine,
Here on earth for years to come,
Not in Heaven, your tasks here done,

Is it selfish to wish it so?
There are so many things I want to know,
I miss you every minute of every day,
What is the reason you couldn't stay?

Take away these chains of sadness,
Open my heart with gladness,
To remember and be grateful for,
The years when I couldn't have asked for more.

Go with God my precious son,
Until my time here is done,
Although we are now physically apart,
You always live within my heart.

One day we will reunite,
In God's garden of infinite light,
Two hearts forever entwined,
Loving you for all time.

The Key That Binds

Your death has taken a heavy toll,
I feel so lost without the role,
Of mother to my wonderful son,
Adviser, friend and companion.

My energy is not the same,
It's slower now and laced with pain,
A heaviness lies within my heart,
Now that we are physically apart.

I am working hard every day,
To understand my life this way,
I am weary and want the faith,
That your death was no mistake.

With God's holy grace,
Take away my heartache,
Only love I want to feel,
Help my broken heart to heal.

To remember and be grateful for,
Every year we had before,
You crossed over to the other side,
In peace and harmony to abide.

Together still, but differently,
Help me to more clearly see,
That we are bound beyond constraints of time,
Because love is the key that binds.

The Song in My Heart

As deep as all the oceans and the seas,
That's what our love meant to me,
As limitless as the skies,
You were the sparkle of joy in my eyes.

Every day was an adventure with you,
I never knew what you would do,
You had brilliant ideas and wonderful plans,
We were looking forward to seeing firsthand.

With movie star looks and the greatest smile,
You were my handsome golden child,
An ambitious young man pursuing your dreams,
With your artistic vision as the means.

Some days I feel strong,
Others like I'm barely hanging on,
Having you die before I do,
Is an anguish I can't believe I'm going through.

I was beside you every step of your way,
You brought joy to my world each day,
A mother loving her dearest son and friend,
Never imagining our time would end.

You are the song in my heart,
Death cannot keep us apart,
I will celebrate you until the day I die,
When we will never again say good-bye.

Thoughts of You

When in grief so very deep,
I often wonder how to keep,
The sense of joy I used to have,
When life did not seem so bad.

Your smiles, your laugh, your handsome face,
Are always there for me to trace,
No matter what I do each day,
Thoughts of you always stay.

Precious boy, unlimited joy,
You were a gift to treasure forever,
Time and space will not replace,
The love that was ours to discover.

When I Learned That You Had Died

When I learned that you had died,
I was numb inside,
I was in disbelief, I didn't cry,
I just couldn't fathom why.

Just that morning we were on the phone,
Talking about plans for coming home,
You were only an hour away,
I said next weekend would be okay.

The previous weekend you'd been here,
It was wonderful you lived so near,
Many college students live far away,
But you could always come home and stay.

What a gift that was for us,
We never had to adjust,
To you being much too far,
To ever get to you by car.

You were home for all occasions,
Adding to the celebrations,
For being young and twenty-two,
We had the most possible time that we could have with you.

I wonder now if that was planned,
As compensation by a divine hand,
Knowing that you were never meant to be,
Here for the years we thought you'd be.

The pain is beyond what I can say,
Ever since you passed away,
So many moments are bittersweet,
With our family now incomplete.

Within my heart there is a hole,
That travels to my very soul,
I pray that in victory we will meet,
Not in agony and defeat.

So I work hard each day,
To remember with thankfulness and praise,
Every year we had with you,
And all the joy and love we knew.

Within My Heart

I think about you when I go to bed at night,
I think about you with the morning light,
I think about you throughout the day,
You are always only a thought away.

Death took you physically,
But otherwise you are still with me,
Love does not disappear,
Because you are no longer here.

You are me and I am you,
Nothing can separate us two,
Although on earth we are now apart,
You live forever within my heart.

Without You

Losing a child feels totally wrong,
I am working hard to be strong,
I love all of my family,
But there is an empty place inside of me.

Just to make it through each day,
Is more agonizing than I can say,
Why, God, does this have to be,
Is there something greater for me to see?

So much of my life was built around you,
Isn't that normal for a mother to do?
I was focused on helping you progress,
As your mother, wanting your best.

There was such satisfaction in watching you grow,
A special young man for everyone to know,
Your happiness gave me great joy,
It's what I hoped for the most, my precious boy.

I know in Heaven there are no worries or stress,
And that you are filled with great happiness,
While I am human and still living here,
I just wish that you were near.

I miss you every minute,
Life's so hard without you in it,
I pray this pain will one day end,
And I will feel joy once again.

The Greatest Sorrow

❦

Give sorrow words. The grief that does not speak Whispers the o'er-fraught heart, and bids it break.

William Shakespeare

A Child's Death

The most unfathomable loss,
Beyond any cost,
Against nature and all comprehension,
A child's death has no explanation.

Our role as a parent is to nurture and protect,
How could we ever suspect,
That despite all our love and care,
Death would come unaware.

It doesn't matter how young or old,
Parents never imagine to lose this hold,
Your child shouldn't die before you do,
Where is the world we thought we knew?

Walking a path forged by pain and sorrow,
Searching for peace in tomorrow,
With faith and acceptance in a divine plan,
I pray I come to understand.

A New Reality

I wish I could have the life I had before,
You walked through Heaven's door,
Instead, I have a new reality,
I have become a different me.

Added cords of pain and grief,
Woven with the tears I weep,
Children shouldn't die before parents do,
It's a living hell to go through.

A brutal severing, a crushing blow,
It goes against everything we know,
Life's fabric is torn apart,
Leaving us with broken hearts.

I know that love never ends,
But I would give anything to see you again,
This sadness never goes away,
Sorrow is with me every day.

A Path Paved With Tears

Anyone who has lost a child can tell,
What it's like to be in Hell,
Torment becomes a part of you,
A new familiar in all you do.

As we struggle through the years,
Our path is paved with many tears,
We pray that we will find relief,
From this pain of constant grief.

If we are lucky in our family and friends,
They share their love to help us mend,
But often focused on issues of their own,
They leave us feeling even more alone.

Most people do not reach out,
Not caring or thinking how they can help,
A simple "I'm sorry," or "I think about you,"
Is more than they can manage to do.

Our children's names are seldom spoken,
Which makes us even more heartbroken,
Because our children are not physically here,
Doesn't make them any less dear.

We all need to think about love and sharing,
And ways to show compassion and caring,
A warm hug, or a caring smile,
Help make life feel more worthwhile.

If we learn to open our hearts,
Realizing we are all a part,
Of a common greater whole,
Love would nourish our souls.

A Trial By Fire

Every day since you've been gone,
I wonder how I keep going on,
How much pain can one endure?
I can barely stand this torture.

A life sentence, there is no escape,
Nothing that could ever equate,
To the loss of a child,
It makes you feel wild.

Crying and screaming,
Internally bleeding,
Blindly grasping for life once more,
But it will never be as it was before.

The sadness never goes away,
It just varies through the days,
From mild to moderate to achingly deep,
Nothing really brings relief.

A trial by fire,
Propelling me higher,
If I can in submission,
Make this transition.

Without the faith that there is a reason,
A purpose to every season,
I would always wonder why,
And wish that I too could die.

So I struggle every day,
Praying for help to find my way,
Opening my heart and my mind,
To the peace that I may find.

Hold me, God, in the palm of your hand,
With heavenly blessings to understand,
That physical death is not the end,
And in love we will all transcend.

An Unknown Road

I long to know why I am here,
It would be wonderful for this to be clear,
No more fumbling around in the dark,
Feeling like my life is in park.

Shine the light so I might drive,
Feeling joy in being alive,
Time has been long and sober,
Ever since you crossed over.

No longer sure of my destination,
When life changed with no explanation,
I now travel an unknown road,
Please take from me this heavy load.

Show me that which I seek,
As I live week to week,
Searching for the inner core,
To feel love and light and joy once more.

Angelversary

The twenty second of September,
Is a day I don't wish to remember,
But I can now never forget,
The date of my child's death.

Whenever September is mentioned,
My thoughts go straight to Heaven,
With trembling lips and tear-filled eyes,
My heart aches for my son who died.

Children's anniversaries should be of marriage,
Occasions of joy and memories to cherish,
It's unimaginable now to me,
To only have our son's angelversary.

It is with the power of the love we knew,
We somehow manage to make it through,
But the anguish within for a child who has passed,
Stays with parents until we breathe our last.

Another Spring

Spring is a time of awakening,
But when your heart is breaking,
There is a poignancy to this season,
Difficulty finding the reason,
To appreciate the birds now singing,
The signs of life the sun is bringing,
The budding trees,
The fresh new leaves.

The flowers are lovely, the breeze is mild,
But I don't have my child,
It's hard to get past the pain,
To focus on what was gained,
I want my heart to be filled with love,
And grateful remembrances of,
All the activities and the things,
That we would do each spring.

Your March birthday memories,
The fun Easter Sundays,
Special times we'll forever recall,
As a family enjoying them all,
The bonds of love will always stay,
Time can never take love away,
I am learning to build my life anew,
With every precious memory of you.

Catapulted Into Grief

My entire world came crashing down,
In seconds, without a sound,
The morning we received a call,
That you had died in a fall.

I was stunned, shocked, in disbelief,
Catapulted into grief,
We had just been on the phone,
Making plans for you to come home.

I felt as if I'd been attacked,
Like a knife was in my back,
I could feel my heart literally breaking,
As I sat, torn and aching.

So many dreams were destroyed,
When you died, my precious boy,
A future without you to share,
Is more than I think I can bear.

Our family is forever changed,
Everything is rearranged,
How do I go on without you,
And all the love that we knew?

Choose Love

How do you measure grief,
However long or brief?
For whatever time we have to treasure,
There is no way for this to measure.

Whether infant, child, teenager, or senior,
Whatever the time that we linger,
There is no way to compare,
Another person's despair.

We can choose to stay broken and bitter,
But we must consider,
In choosing this instead of love,
We block the healing from above.

With a divine team on the other side,
Our loved ones watch and gently guide,
As we work through our pain and sadness,
Spirit wraps its love around us.

In God's grace I want to live,
In all ways to forgive,
Give me the strength to carry on,
When it feels as if all hope is gone.

Heartache

Sometimes my chest is heavy and I can't breathe,
Everything starts to seize,
My heart hurts and I start to cry,
Wondering why you had to die.

Heartache is not just a term,
As I have sadly come to learn,
It's painful and it's real,
A hurt you pray one day will heal.

So often scars do not show,
Others may never know,
The pain in varying degrees,
That one may carry that we don't see.

Your death has opened my eyes,
To anguish that can be inside,
And how many people there are,
Bearing similar scars.

Loss makes you understand much more,
Than you ever could before,
It rips you open and makes you bleed,
More compassionate to those in need.

Underneath we are all the same,
No one lives without any pain,
Let me in love reach out,
Helping others in darkness and doubt.

Like Yesterday

I may look like I am fine,
When people see me from time to time,
But at any moment I can cry,
Emotions changing in the blink of an eye.

It's been almost a full two years,
Since you were last here,
Yet it seems like only yesterday,
That you passed away.

I still think that you'll come home,
And you will telephone,
Your room is waiting for you,
How can this be true?

Everything feels so surreal,
What is this karmic wheel?
I want to get off this treadmill of pain,
Transforming through spiritual gain.

You were my child, but I must let you go,
Because no one ever owns a soul,
A gift from Heaven for whatever the time,
I was blessed to call you mine.

Love Like No Other

Time heals all wounds they say,
I am waiting for that day,
It's been years and I still cry,
Missing my son who died.

Love between a child and mother,
Is love like no other,
Death cannot sever this bond,
The ties of the heart are much too strong.

The pain may soften a little over time,
But the wound is never left behind,
Forever there will be an ache in my heart,
Sorrow that we must be apart.

I never imagined that he'd not be here,
To love and cherish through the years,
A treasured son I can no longer see,
Held close in loving memory.

Mourning

No one can mourn for you,
It's a process you have to go through,
Working, playing, sleeping or awake,
There is no escape.

I can't wish it away,
Or bring back prior days,
The grief is always sitting there,
And I am constantly aware.

That I will never again see,
The son who meant the world to me,
Adjusting to this devastation,
When my world has lost its foundation.

Is something I could never have imagined,
How could this have happened?
My anchor is no longer here,
The purpose I have not as clear.

Which direction do I go?
It's so hard for me to know,
I just wanted to be your mom,
I can't believe that you are gone.

Stay with me in spirit form,
In new faith I will be born,
The power of love will bring us together,
Because the ties of love can never sever.

No Right or Wrong

There are no shortcuts when in grief,
The wound is much too deep,
Like learning to live without a limb,
Somehow managing to go on,
But always aware of what is gone.

There is no right or wrong way in mourning,
Emotions often give no warning,
One minute functioning normally,
The next minute sobbing uncontrollably.

If one just wants to stay in bed,
Go right ahead,
Don't let people dictate what to do,
They have no idea what we're going through.

For me, there is no greater pain,
Than knowing I won't see my son again,
No longer able to give him my love and care,
Is almost more than I can bear.

Somehow the days go by,
And I can only try,
To slowly build my life anew,
Without the physical presence of you.

I know the body is not the whole,
I just miss you so,
If I could have but one wish,
It would be to have you here to hug and kiss.

A Mother's Tears

Despite the anguish now a part of me,
For the dreams we will not see,
I am grateful for the years,
You enriched our lives while you were here.

I wouldn't trade a single day,
For nothing will ever outweigh,
The unconditional love we knew,
For every moment we had with you.

One More Day Without You

One more day without you,
Somehow time passes by,
One more day without you,
How long does a mother cry?

One more day without you,
The days turn into years,
One more day without you,
Since you last were here.

One more day without you,
The sun is shining bright,
One more day without you,
As the sun fades into night.

One more day without you,
But you are always in my thoughts,
One more day without you,
Holding you in my heart.

One more day without you,
Yet each day turns into the past,
One more day without you,
Then we'll be together at last.

One Step Forward, Two Steps Back

My son's death leaves such a hole,
I feel so lost without my role,
As his mother and his friend,
Will my heartache ever end?

One step forward, two steps back,
Will I ever get back on track?
Help me to find my stride,
With divine love and comfort guide.

Pick me up when I fall,
I want to stand straight and tall,
I know you don't want me on the ground,
With tears of anguish the only sound.

Give me strength to carry on,
These days seem far too long,
I hope in victory we will meet,
Not in agony and defeat.

Other People

I could empathize and sympathize,
Before my son died,
When hearing of other people's losses,
Spouses, siblings, friends, and bosses.

I would be sad,
But of course be so glad,
That it wasn't me,
Undergoing such tragedy.

You never really imagine,
That it could ever happen,
To you or your family,
How could that be?

And then the unthinkable comes true,
The "other people" become you,
And you realize that you never really knew,
What those other people were actually going through.

When your world comes crashing down,
Without a single sound,
You feel as if you're all alone,
When your child will never be coming home.

You could have one child or ten,
It doesn't matter,
When you know that no one can take the place,
Of that one precious child's face.

My life is in pieces,
I pray this anguish eases,
As I work to rebuild my life,
Nothing now feels right.

Focusing on the blessings won,
When God gifted us with our son,
Is what I work to concentrate on,
Now that he is physically gone.

Though our life will never be the same,
The love will forever remain,
So with every breath that I breathe,
My son is still alive with me.

Purpose

I thought that my purpose was being a mother,
I couldn't imagine another,
Greater role for me to play,
I was fulfilled in my days.

In a moment, you were gone,
The structures I relied upon,
Blown apart, a crumpled heap,
Ruins at my feet.

Every day I ask myself,
What is this all about?
I pray for divine clarity,
For greater wisdom to see,
Beyond this world of illusion,
To come to a conclusion.

I know now that purpose isn't limited to one,
There is no certain sum,
There are stages and times,
When purpose realigns.

I feel so lost and confused,
Nothing now is what I knew,
Please God, help me find,
What now is my soul's design.

Searching for You

Praying my heartfelt soul's lament,
I fear my tears will never be spent,
Aching, soul-deep despair and sorrow,
It's so hard to care about tomorrow.

True agony of the soul,
What now will be my goal?
No longer will there be,
The plans and dreams I hoped to see.

I still look for you each day,
How could you have passed away?
I look for you in the house and yard,
Nothing I could imagine would be this hard.

Without the sense that you are here,
Only in a different sphere,
The pain would be much too deep,
For my soul to ever keep.

Stay always by my side,
A loving, helpful spirit guide,
And when my time here has passed,
Together we will be at last.

Sorrow

Sorrow has become a second skin,
I am learning to find acceptance within,
A new layer, an added depth,
Bound by the tears that I've wept.

Unfathomable, the tragic cost,
When your beloved child is lost,
Your heart literally aches,
Torn apart in heartbreak.

Other losses compound this pain,
So many things in my life have changed,
The hopes and dreams I thought would be,
Are gone or laced with uncertainty.

We were almost living a fairy tale,
A beautiful family where all went well,
Our future looked positive and bright,
Filled with happiness and light.

I am a mother with a broken smile,
Who held my children's hands for a while,
One child has died, the other is on her own,
I never thought to be this alone.

Losses make you much more aware,
That everyone has crosses to bear,
I pray daily for God's healing embrace,
Supported in heavenly love and grace.

Tears of Love

Every day the tears still flow,
There is no predicting or control,
No embarrassment or shame,
What is there to blame?

Something said, a song or a thought,
Any number of things can tug my heart,
Tears are a way of cleansing the soul,
Mending us to make us whole.

Every teardrop contains great love,
For the son I am thinking of,
A natural way to honor and respect,
A life and love I'll never forget.

Spirit moves the love we feel,
With energies to soothe and heal,
I am thankful for this release,
Because the tears will lead to peace.

Someday these tears of sadness,
Will transform into tears of gladness,
Because every day I had with you,
Was worth the mourning I am going through.

Nothing can take our love away,
A gift to treasure for all my days,
Love continues, it never dies,
No matter how many tears we cry.

The Broken-Hearted

We are the broken-hearted parents,
Who struggle every day,
Weighted down with sorrow,
For our children who have passed away.

Weary travelers joining many others,
Who are also on this road,
None of us ever imagined,
We'd be carrying this heavy load.

The road is long and filled with anguish,
Flowing with all of our tears,
And the pieces of the dreams we'd envisioned,
With our children through the years.

In a club no one wants to join,
Screaming silently all the way,
We can't believe how our lives have changed,
And the price we have to pay.

Sometimes we wish we could cross over,
That we too could die,
The pain is almost unbearable,
And all we do is cry.

We listen for our children's voices,
And feel so terribly alone,
It's unimaginable living without them,
We just want our children home.

If only it were possible,
There's nothing we wouldn't do,
To be together once again,
Would be a dream come true.

We know they're happy in Heaven,
Waiting for us to come,
The only consolation,
Until our time here is done.

We may not have the answers,
Or understand the plan,
But we are very thankful,
To have held their precious hands.

We're separated physically,
In that way we're apart,
But in all other ways still connected,
Forever within our hearts.

We cherish every moment,
And are grateful through our tears,
To have known the love of our children,
And for the time that they were here.

To have been their parents is a blessing,
And though our hearts are torn,
We hope to celebrate their memory,
And not forever mourn.

The love we had was priceless,
In it we rejoice,
And if we had the chance again,
We would make no other choice.

The Saddest Words

The saddest words I can ever say,
Are that I had a son, but he passed away,
No one, however aware,
Can imagine the pain that I now bear.

Why would this be assigned,
To me in this lifetime?
How could I ever choose to part,
With the treasure of my heart?

There is nothing that will ever fix,
A world that's been blown to bits,
One day all you thought to be true,
No longer applies to you.

A wake up call,
That takes your all,
And leaves you screaming,
Searching for meaning.

My life is all asunder,
But I don't want to go under,
I'm grasping for the lifeline,
To make it through this time.

Shall I sink or shall I swim?
I don't know where to begin,
Sometimes I'd like to float away,
Not having to struggle another day.

Now my inner self is coming out,
Helping to remove fear and doubt,
So I take another stroke,
Gradually moving toward the hope.

That in time the seas will calm,
And I will find the balm,
Because everything that I need,
Is really right inside of me.

The Strike of a Clock

Death came suddenly while I was asleep,
On unobserved silent feet,
I didn't know when I went to bed,
In the morning I'd learn you were dead.

At fifty-two with the strike of a clock,
The life I knew came to a stop,
One little movement of a clock's hands,
Ended your precious life span.

Each day now is a struggle to get through,
It's as if half of me went with you,
Your young life was far too brief,
How does a mother live with this grief?

There is no answer for this question,
I can only pray the pain will lessen,
And that all thoughts will be of joy,
For the gift of my cherished boy.

Unintentional Hurt

It's almost unbearable to have your child pass away,
It's excruciating to get through each day,
When so much reason for living is gone,
It's all we can do just to hold on.

Well-meaning relatives and friends,
Oftentimes unknowingly offend,
With things that they say or don't do,
With insensitivity dealing with you.

Just under the surface always are tears,
We never know when they'll appear,
It's alright for us to cry,
Even if others don't understand why.

People are uncomfortable thinking about our walk,
So they don't want to have any talk,
Not realizing acting as if our child didn't exist,
Is like having our heart hit by a fist.

Without experiencing a child's loss yourself,
Most people don't know how to help,
They think we should go on as if before,
Our children walked through Heaven's door.

They question our focus on our departed ones,
Because they have no comprehension,
Of how our world has profoundly changed,
And that we can never be the same.

The Greatest Sorrow

For the rest of our lives we will live with sorrow,
For the loss of our children and the dreams of tomorrow,
We want to keep their memory alive,
It's what helps us to survive.

People need to learn to be more forgiving,
There's no less love for the living,
Love is not finite, it goes on forever,
And as parents we will always remember.

Unrelenting Grief

After my son died,
I just cried and cried,
I didn't know what to do with myself,
Or where I could turn for help.

My mind wouldn't stop,
I was aware every minute of my loss,
Years ago I liked to knit,
In desperation I turned back to it.

I knit an afghan, some scarves and hats,
It helped quiet my mind and to relax,
A lifeline of relief,
A respite from the grief.

A brainwave change, a form of meditation,
I was so grateful for any cessation,
Of the unrelenting sorrow and ache,
Of my total heartbreak.

A year later I am not as driven,
To be constantly knitting,
I joined a yoga class that meets each week,
Looking for healing and inner peace.

I meditate every morning and pray,
And I look for signs that say,
I love you mom, I am here,
Feel my presence, always near.

The Greatest Sorrow

I believe my son is part of a heavenly team,
Working hard from heights unseen,
To help me as I grieve,
So I will be open to receive.

Blessings that I might find,
If I can clear my mind,
And surrender into my heart,
With the love of which we are all a part.

The Circle of Family and Home

❦

Family above all else.

Graham Stevenson
2006

Family above all else.

This phrase likely means nothing to many, but I derive great hope and pleasure from its message. Your sacrifice, love, and ever-enduring will to see this family succeed and thrive is what bolsters my confidence in this ideal. As each year passes I find myself filled with increasing gratitude for your love and support. Beyond this day of honor towards all mothers, I hope through my actions and accomplishments to daily celebrate your contribution to this family. The values you have instilled in me, the love you have shown us all, and the (at times) incomprehensible patience you have demonstrated as I grew are all integral parts of who I have become and without them much, if not all, of what I have done would not be possible. By placing your family above all else you have exemplified the power and necessity of love and provided me with the faith necessary to live a good and productive life in a terribly flawed and frightening world. Thank you for all that you have done, I will be forever grateful.

Happy Mother's Day

I love and appreciate you very much!

Graham

Graham wrote this as his gift to me for Mother's Day 2006. He was twenty-one years old. Sixteen months after writing this Graham died. The original is framed and hanging on my bedroom wall. I will always treasure these written words from Graham's heart. Thank you, Graham, I love you.

A Deafening Silence

How empty this house now seems,
Without you as part of its dreams,
The silence is deafening,
Where is the lessening,
Of a grief so deep, it seeps,
Into the very walls,
And yet recalls,
The echoes of the happiness,
When you were still with us,
So on higher notes, this love transcends,
The pain when it again descends,
And gently lifts our souls once more,
With memories of our love and gratefulness for,
Every moment that we knew,
With the blessing that was you.

A Different World

We've lived in our house four and a half years,
But it feels as if I just moved here,
I wonder why it doesn't seem so long,
And realize it's because you are gone.

Two years ago you passed away,
In some ways time seems to have stopped that day,
If only your death weren't true,
And life could be the way we knew.

It feels as if I am waiting,
That I am anticipating,
Your return from parts unknown,
That you will soon be coming home.

It's like a movie, how can this be?
I want to deny the reality,
And see you walking in the door,
Home to visit us once more.

My tears still fall every day,
I never imagined my world this way,
I'll miss you until the day I die,
When there'll be no more need to cry.

A Gift of Love

Six months after our son passed away,
Was our daughter's wedding day,
The plans had already been in place,
For us all to anticipate.

Our son had planned to design her invitations,
His gift for this joyous occasion,
His graphic design skills would have meant so much,
Giving our daughter's day an extra special touch.

A gift of love from his heart,
That he was unable to start,
And though he wasn't physically there,
His presence was felt everywhere.

Our son's death was so tragic,
But the wedding had a feeling of magic,
People commented on the love they felt,
The sense of family and joy throughout.

Looking back I wonder how I got things done,
And realize it was with the help of my son,
With the aid of a heavenly team,
To help us still realize a wedding day dream.

A House of Broken Dreams

A house of boards and beams,
Built with so many hopes and dreams,
A family endeavor in which we all had our parts,
A vision so dear to our hearts.

Like waiting for a baby to come,
It took nine months until the house was done,
It was so exciting to wait for the day,
We could move in and stay.

For two and a half years we enjoyed the house,
Your presence is felt throughout,
But one morning as you waved good-bye,
So many of our dreams suddenly died.

It's been several years now that you've been gone,
And the emptiness stretches on,
In a home now of broken dreams,
Nothing is as it seems.

We never know what the years will hold,
A child is more precious than gold,
When you died a part of us died too,
And everything changed from what we knew.

A Mother's Dreams

As a baby at my breast,
I promised you my very best,
You gave my life so much meaning,
Fulfilled hopes that I'd been dreaming.

Every little baby smile,
Made my life so worthwhile,
There was so much joy,
Having you as my little boy.

Lullabies and nursery rhymes,
Children's songs and playtimes,
Your favorite blanket and all your toys,
There was so much that we enjoyed.

As you grew,
The joys grew too,
Of course there were difficult times,
But we were able to find.

Our love would always overcome,
What had been troublesome,
I never thought I'd have to say,
I had a son but he passed away.

At twenty-two your thoughts and plans,
Were so very close at hand,
The future you envisioned,
Never to come to fruition.

Eight months short of graduation,
We were planning for the celebration,
The culmination of years of studies,
Perseverance, ideas and worries.

I mourn for the future that will never be,
But rejoice in the gift you were to me,
For every day you were here on earth,
From the moment I gave you birth.

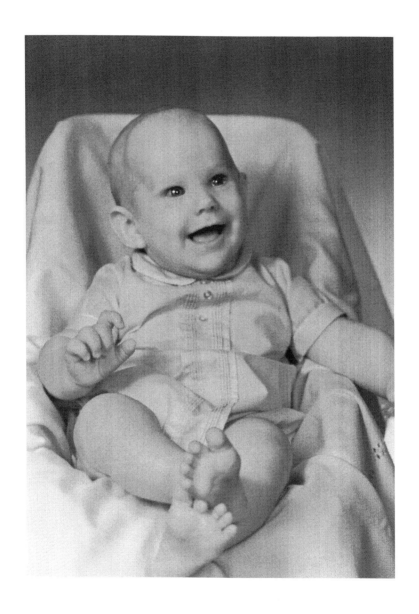

A Mother's Tears

I have cried a river of tears,
This past year,
I know that I am not alone,
So many others called home,
All of our tears mingle,
They are never single,
United in our grief,
Struggling to find relief.

I pray the tears cleanse my soul,
Mend the hole,
That now is in my life,
Take away the strife.

Divine Spirit fill the gloom,
So that I may bloom,
With spiritual eyes,
To realize,
That what affects one, affects another.

There are so many mothers,
With empty arms and crying eyes,
Asking God, why?
Help us find the peace we seek,
To live our lives to teach,
That family is a treasure,
And that love is forever.

This poem inspired the title of this book. The poem grew from my thoughts about all of the tears that I cried following the death of my son, and my realization that there are so many mothers who are also crying rivers of tears over the loss of their children.

Cherish Your Happy Moments

I don't know what to do,
With my life without you,
It's so hard after twenty-two years,
To live on without you here.

As your mother why would I,
Imagine that you would die?
It's a sorrow no parent should know,
Unimaginable to let you go.

Is it true with the divine,
That no one dies before their time?
No accidents, no tragedies,
That we all die when it's meant to be?

People shouldn't assume they'll grow old,
Or know how their life will unfold,
At any moment things can change,
Never think it's all arranged.

Cherish the happy moments and hold them fast,
So the beautiful memories will always last,
Honor loved ones and hold them dear,
With gratefulness and joy for every year.

Circle of Love

Minutes to hours to days to weeks,
Months to years, time slowly creeps,
It's still hard to believe that you are not here,
That doesn't change whatever the year.

We thought you would marry and bring home a wife,
Adding another dimension to our life,
We hoped there would be your children to hold,
A circle of family more precious than gold.

These dreams with you we will not see,
None of them meant to be,
We have to treasure the years that we shared,
Remembering how much we all cared.

A beautiful family built on a foundation of love,
That we were all blessed to be a part of,
We may never understand why you are gone,
Or why the rest of us have to live on.

But we will keep your memory alive,
With all of the love we hold inside,
Cherishing every moment that we had together,
You will live in our hearts forever.

Forgotten you will never be,
Forever integral to our family,
Our circle of love will once more unite,
When we join together in God's holy light.

Family Tree Afghan

Every day seated on my couch,
I wrap an afghan all about,
Upon the afghan a family tree,
With the names of my husband, daughter, son, and me.

The roots of the tree are the mother and father,
The branches hold our son and daughter,
Two generations, a family of four,
Nothing could ever mean any more.

Two years ago our son died,
After twenty-two years in our lives,
A day never passes without any tears,
Missing our son for the rest of our years.

The family tree is not the same,
There will be no continuation of our name,
How can our son be gone?
Everything now feels so wrong.

Moving through unimaginable pain,
I work on enjoying life again,
Comforted in my afghan of memories and love,
Grateful for the years we were all a part of.

The afghan helps me feel our son is close by,
And to remember that love never dies,
You cannot separate a branch from the tree,
Forever we will be a family.

Father's Day

Another Father's Day is here,
The second one without you here,
Two years ago I had saved,
The card for your dad that you gave.

I got it out for your dad again,
To read and feel the love it sends,
We remember your last Father's Day,
Happy that summer you were able to stay.

Your father and I are so proud of you,
We think of you in all we do,
Incomprehensible that you are gone,
We are doing our best to carry on.

An amazing young man and cherished son,
You filled our world with adventure and fun,
We are so grateful to have been your mom and dad,
And for every moment that we had.

Finding My Way

What is the roadmap for my soul?
I would dearly love to know,
So much sorrow I hold within,
I don't know where to begin.

Starting life over after losing you,
Is the most painful thing I must do,
I am left here on earth weeping,
For part of my heart is now in your keeping.

A mother grieving her dearest son,
With no idea how it's done,
Every day is a test,
I want my soul to be at rest.

Somehow I will see this through,
What else is there for me to do?
Show me the guideposts to follow each day,
As I struggle to find my way.

Mother's Day

I woke up feeling sad today,
I know it's because of Mother's Day,
Two years ago you were here,
Sharing the day with family near.

We have beautiful pictures of you and me,
Mother and son, we were so happy,
How proud I was of you,
My handsome son of twenty-two.

I thought that we had forever,
But as the family gathers together,
There will be an empty space,
That no one can ever replace.

I wish with all my heart,
That we were not apart,
I want to see you physically,
To laugh and talk and be with me.

I miss you more than one could know,
And every day I strive to show,
Although our years were far too few,
I was blessed to be the mother of you.

Mothers

Poets through the ages have tried to express,
The unconditional love that mothers show best,
Searching for words that capture the emotion,
Of a mother's endless care and devotion.

Their nature is to nurture, to love and protect,
A mother could never do any less,
It is their love that provides the stepping stone,
For their children to launch and come into their own.

Their wisdom and guidance will never steer you wrong,
Children are a mother's heart song,
Selfless and dedicated to their families,
Beautiful models of what to be.

A wonderful mother is one of life's greatest gifts,
Her presence never fails to uplift,
No human is perfect, but mothers come close,
That is why children love them the most.

I think this is part of God's design,
Because life has many difficult times,
Mothers help us to not feel alone,
And provide comfort and security in the unknown.

Thank you for the blessing of mothers,
For their love is like no other,
Value all moments and treasure,
A love that has no measure.

Night Sky

My husband and I,
Sleep underneath a beautiful night sky,
Painted on the ceiling above our bed,
As we gaze directly overhead.

A September sky with a lovely full moon,
And shining stars that fill up our room,
The Aries constellation is painted there too,
Our son's Zodiac sign for us to view.

The sky as it was on the night he died,
Painted by his friend with an artistic eye,
With a line from a poem painted on one end,
A memorial written by my dear friend.

It comforts me as I go to sleep at night,
And when I wake with the morning light,
Our son is never very far,
Our bright and shining golden star.

A month before Graham died, I had spoken with him about the possibility of his friend, Jack Currier, a talented artist, painting some sort of scene on the tray ceiling in our bedroom. Graham said Jack would do a good job for us. After Graham died while walking on a beautiful September night, I knew that the ceiling scene should show the night sky that he enjoyed on his walk. I wanted to feel surrounded by that night sky, with many stars and the bright full moon. Jack captured that perfectly in the scene he painted on the ceiling. That moon and star-filled sky helps to keep Graham close as his love shines down upon us. Shortly after Graham's death, my dear friend Vivian wrote this poem for us. The last line of her poem was a perfect caption for the scene. We thank Jack and Vivian for these invaluable gifts of love.

Graham

He was a bright and shining star,
I could see his reflection in your eyes,
Now he runs across the night,
His magic lights up the skies.

Vivian West
2007

Our Home

I have lived in many places, near and far to roam,
But I am happy now to be able to stay at home,
To own a house was a dream come true,
A place for all the family to come to.

No more moving, everyone in the same state,
So much joy to anticipate,
With much thought and deliberation,
I worked hard to create a haven.

I pictured my daughter and my son,
Meeting and marrying that special someone,
And sharing holidays and many occasions,
In a home filled with love and celebration.

A new phase of life when childhood ends,
As young adults your children become friends,
So many hopes and expectations,
Were suddenly gone with no explanation.

At twenty-two our son died,
In an instant with no good-bye,
So many plans for the future are gone,
And the emptiness without him stretches on.

So grateful that we bought this house,
Our son's presence is all about,
As a graphic designer he had a keen eye,
And gave us many ideas to try.

From the pattern of the kitchen floor,
To the color of our front door,
Suggestions on which cabinets to choose,
We loved to hear his views.

In the yard he planted his apple trees,
The ones he grew from seeds,
Flowers and bushes he helped select and grow,
So many gifts of love to know.

The house is my sanctuary and retreat,
It's filled with my son's spirit sweet,
And the many remembrances of,
The ways in which he showed his love.

Sweet Little Tammy

Our sweet little Tammy dog,
Is laid to rest in our backyard,
Beside my son's apple tree,
The perfect place for her to be.

My son and Tammy were very fond,
Of each other and shared a bond,
And when my son planted his trees,
Tammy was there enjoying the breeze.

Eighteen months ago my son passed away,
And three weeks ago Tammy was placed in her grave,
A birthday present fifteen years ago,
For my children to love and know.

A dog's life span is not very long,
We knew that one day she would be gone,
But the shock of a child dying before your dog,
Seems impossible to be allowed.

From my window I can see Tammy's grave,
And I remember the love that she gave,
It's comforting to know that she and my son,
Are together again having fun.

I am working on being happy for all of the years,
That we had together and not the tears,
Because the love and memories live inside of me,
Held close and cherished with the years left to be.

Tammy

Today we had to put to sleep,
Our darling little Sheltie, so sweet,
A part of our family for fifteen years,
She enriched our lives while she was here.

She was the best a dog could be,
With a delightful personality,
Happy and loving, patient and kind,
A pleasure to have for all this time.

Her favorite thing was to eat,
She especially liked a treat,
She would gladly lie down, shake or sit,
To get a favorite little bit.

She liked to walk in the snow,
And to feel the wind blow,
She would lift her head to the breeze,
Content and happy as you please.

She would follow me around the house,
Wanting to see what I was about,
Lying beside a favorite chair,
Or tucked up against the stairs.

Always such good company,
A part of our family,
From everyday times to special occasions,
She was always part of the celebrations.

We miss her and appreciate,
All our moments small and great,
With our wonderful companion and devoted friend,
She leaves us memories that will never end.

Traces of You

I almost assume,
When I look in your room,
That you will be standing there,
Alive and aware.

I look at your bed,
Where you last laid your head,
Your scent still lingers there,
A faint trace in the air.

I hug your pillow and wish that it was you,
Crying and saying, our moments were too few,
A room now holding only memories,
Of all the dreams we hoped to see.

Your artwork is on your walls,
Beautiful photographs to remind us all,
Of how fortunate we were while you were here,
How you brightened so many of our years.

Now my world feels destroyed,
How do I fill the void?
The future is not what I thought it would be,
Time seems to stretch endlessly.

Building a life anew,
Is an agonizing process to go through,
Anything else in life seems mild,
In comparison to losing your child.

Love is the answer to every question we scream,
Love is for what we dream,
I pray for love in all its forms,
Because it is in love that we are reborn.

I know that this is true,
Walking this path through the loss of you,
The sacrifice on both our parts,
Will lead to opening our hearts.

Let me feel the universal flow,
To come to know,
That love cannot be divided,
When in spirit we are forever united.

Unsatisfying Phrases

"He's in a better place,"
As if that can erase,
The loss of a loved one's sweet embrace,
Or the sight of that precious face.

"We can't know,"
Goes to show,
How little these phrases satisfy,
We do want to know, "why?"

Consciousness risen,
Answers be given,
To the journey of a soul,
This is my goal.

With an open heart and an open mind,
I pray that I may find,
What was lost,
At the greatest cost.

To be able to release,
And to find the peace,
The comfort, the surety,
That all is as it's meant to be.

Wondering Why

When I am in that twilight state,
Half asleep and half awake,
On fully awakening there are times I find,
I am saying my poetry in my mind.

Sometimes I realize that I am crying,
Grief always present with my son dying,
In this sadness I start the day,
It's harder than I could ever say.

I don't know why this has to be,
So little now makes sense to me,
Somehow I manage to go on,
Praying for peace with each new dawn.

Finding Comfort in Loss

⟨⟨✶⟩⟩

Blessed are they that mourn: for they shall be comforted.

Matthew 5:4 (King James Version)

A Brighter Tomorrow

Help my sorrow to release,
So I may find inner peace,
Take away my cries and tears,
Remove from me all doubts and fears,

I want to walk in the light,
To make it through this dark night,
To find happiness in being alive,
Even though my son has died.

Does this pain ever go away?
Will it gradually ease each day?
There's not a moment you are separate from me,
Together always, in memory.

In this way there is no death,
Because you live in every breath,
A physical change, but not of the soul,
The spirit remains vibrant and whole.

With Heaven's aid and direction,
I still feel our love and connection,
Supporting me in this terrible sorrow,
With the faith to believe in a brighter tomorrow.

A Gift From Heaven

Thank you for the poetry,
That has begun flowing through me,
I know it's from deep within myself,
I'm so grateful for this angelic help.

The words bring some sweet relief,
To all these months of constant grief,
A sense of satisfaction too,
Because I feel more attuned with you.

I hope to share these poems with others,
There are so many fathers and mothers,
Who have also had a child die,
And are desperately wondering why.

Maybe these words of mine,
Will help soothe their pain for a time,
Comfort that I can impart,
To help mend a broken heart.

The words help me also as I learn to heal,
With what still feels so unreal,
Nothing will ever take the pain away,
But I think it softens day by day.

As life continues and we go on,
Without that precious physical bond,
We begin to more clearly see,
That we are not our earthly body.

Our loved ones never go away,
They are present in a different way,
And with an open heart and an open mind,
What we think is lost, we find.

I am so grateful to have this connection,
Of love and grace giving direction,
With comfort and validation, knowing within,
That physical death is not the end.

A Message From My Son

In the arms of the angels I was flown,
Back to my heavenly home,
It came as a surprise to me,
But this is how it's supposed to be.

I am happy, do not weep,
Love is forever ours to keep,
Now I work from this side,
As one of your spirit guides.

So alone I know you feel,
But I am present to help you heal,
I send you love and many signs,
As you struggle through this dark time.

I know your heart is broken,
But with divine love it will open,
And from what feels like tragedy,
You'll be able to more clearly see.

The plans God has in store for you,
A purpose that will come shining through,
Keep the faith, don't give in,
A new life will begin.

I want you to know,
That I love you so,
And I watch with pride,
As you find your stride.

Although my earthly life is done,
I am so grateful to be your son,
And in Heaven I await,
The time you'll walk through God's gate.

In the meantime do not fear,
Know that I am always near,
Feel the heavenly support from above,
For the mother that I so dearly love.

Thank you, Graham, for the miracle of this poem.

Celestial Realms

You can now be found,
In Heaven's celestial realms,
No longer bound by earthly cares,
Trouble-free and light as air.

Happy, and where you are meant to be,
In the plan of eternity,
Having made that highest climb,
Living in joy sublime.

I envy you your new birth,
It's hard living on this earth,
And with you no longer here,
My days are filled with many tears.

I am trusting in a divine plan,
Believing our lives are in God's hands,
Finding faith to persevere,
Praying life's meaning becomes more clear.

I want to be happy too,
Even though I can't be with you,
You are with me in other ways,
I feel your presence every day.

Run amidst the moon and stars,
We are together wherever we are,
Love can't be measured by hours or minutes,
Love has no boundaries, love has no limits.

Count Your Blessings

Count your blessings large and small,
Be thankful for them all,
A beautiful day, a note from a friend,
Your pet's happy greeting, the list never ends.

The love of your family, a baby's smile,
So many things make life worthwhile,
When at night you go to bed,
Make a list inside your head.

What did your day bring?
Think of any positive thing,
Let the shadows move and pass,
Dark clouds do not always last.

Look for the sun, for it will rise,
Let no negative visions obscure the eyes,
Ask for any heavenly help,
To move beyond thoughts of self.

Cherish every happy memory and know,
That we are here to learn and grow,
And that if we walk each day in love,
All our needs will be taken care of.

Do Not Cry

Close your eyes and go to sleep,
I am with you mother, do not weep,
Place your hand upon your heart,
My hand is there too, never apart.

Feel the love I have for you,
And the strength to see you through,
I am with you every day,
Helping you to find your way.

No more sorrow, smile for me,
I want to see you living happily,
Our love is forever, love doesn't die,
Please mother, do not cry.

Remember our years with joy and smiles,
Every moment was so worthwhile,
Only partially separated for a brief time,
Our hearts remain forever entwined.

Don't Give In

I look at pictures now of me,
And don't recognize the face I see,
The spark of life, of joy is gone,
I look tired and drawn.

I sometimes envision blood dripping from my wrists,
Wondering why I exist,
What is the point of my life now?
With my child dying, it doesn't matter somehow.

The meaning is no longer clear,
Of what I am doing here,
Even my little dog passed away,
Nothing in life can ever stay.

Physical forms all turn to dust,
While we struggle to adjust,
Searching for the eternal core,
To understand what we came here for.

With the promise of love eternal,
Like a ring you encircle,
Surrounding me and knowing just when,
To whisper to me, don't give in.

I listen for your beloved voice,
Anticipating the day I'll rejoice,
No longer bound by earthly cares,
I will be made fully aware.

Of what was learned and what was gained,
From every earthly joy and pain,
My spirit will be set free,
At one with eternity.

Help me make it day by day,
The time seems so far away,
I want to be open to receive,
Heavenly gifts that are sent to me.

Fragile Wings of Hope

When the anguish of loss begins to soften,
When the pain is not as often,
You slowly begin to emerge,
From the darkness in which submerged.

Like a baby taking his first step,
Moving beyond the tears you've wept,
You tentatively venture forward once more,
Opening a new and different door.

Fragile wings of hope and healing,
That maybe life can still be appealing,
Start to flutter in your heart,
As you seek a new start.

Wondering if you can find meaning again,
With hope that a soul can mend,
With the love that we knew,
I am praying for this to be true.

God's Garden

You are in God's garden,
With Jesus and all the saints,
Side by side with angels,
Shining in God's holy grace.

In a kingdom filled with glory,
And joy and eternal light,
Imbued with brilliant colors,
That inspire and delight.

A soul at peace in Heaven,
Having journeyed home again,
No more trials and tribulations,
Those have come to an end.

With love beyond imagining,
No selfishness or strife,
Only harmony and peace abounding,
In everlasting life.

Our love is forever,
I know you wait for me,
I'll join you in God's garden,
When it's my time to see.

God's Promise

God promises that one day our tears will be wiped away,
Help me to have faith this anguish won't stay,
When broken-hearted and crushed with sorrow,
It hurts too much to think of tomorrow.

Just making it through each day,
Is more difficult than I can say,
The emptiness without you here,
Is beyond my darkest fear.

Why did God call your name?
Nothing will ever be the same,
I just assumed that you would always be,
In this world as a part of me.

My beloved son and treasured friend,
Your body died, but that's not the end,
Holy Spirit, Infinite Light,
With love and compassion, renew my sight.

God's Time

The days are turning into years,
Since the time you last were here,
It doesn't seem like that much time has passed,
When we were able to see you last.

You are now beyond our physical touch,
But in our hearts loved so much,
Why did you have to go?
There are so many things I don't know.

What can ever take this pain away?
It's so hard living with sorrow each day,
Sometimes I tire of being here,
I pray for my purpose to become more clear.

Sweet angels of mercy, healing, and grace,
Comfort me in your loving embrace,
Help me learn to let go,
And to discover the gifts of my soul.

Let me surrender to the peace of the divine,
Accepting that all is in God's time,
Give me faith that one day I'll be,
Walking in love and harmony.

Heal the wounds of my heart,
Mend the jagged, aching parts,
Remembering with every breath,
That ultimately there is no death.

We will be together again,
When my earthly time comes to an end,
Two souls united once more,
When I too enter Heaven's door.

Healing Waters

Sea salt baths and lavender scents,
All of these are meant,
To soothe the body, soul, and mind,
Please, let them heal mine.

I turn to these in my distress,
Hoping the pain will become less,
I read, I pray, I meditate,
Every day I contemplate.

To find some reason when all without,
Leaves me in confusion and doubt,
I miss you son, I love you so,
Why was it your time to go?

I am doing the best I can,
To have faith in a master plan,
As I slowly work through this agony of grief,
Praying for help and relief.

Jewelry of Comfort

Every day as I dress,
Going through my jewelry I select,
Bracelets, necklaces, and earrings,
For whatever comfort they might bring.

Like putting on a suit of armor,
They provide protection and honor,
All the memories I have of you,
And the bond of love that we knew.

I have jewelry with crystals to soothe and to heal,
Angels and Madonnas with their love to feel,
Winged things representing the signs,
You send to me in many designs.

Beautiful dragonflies in different colors,
Butterflies to softly flutter,
Hummingbirds to dangle from my ears,
All worn with bittersweet tears.

Jewelry about being a mom,
Lord, help me to be strong,
I am trying my best,
But every day is a test.

I have a bracelet with the Lord's Prayer,
Inspirational necklaces with verses of love and care,
A gold shooting star that represents your life,
Bright and shining, but only briefly in sight.

Finding Comfort in Loss

Hearts that show the love,
Of a son I thought the world of,
Small comforts to help me face,
What time will never erase.

Because no matter how long we cry,
A mother's love will never die,
Like the mother-child ring that I wear each day,
Nothing can take this bond away.

I never used to wear much jewelry. After my son died, I needed to feel connected to him in a tangible way. Jewelry with special meaning, as I describe in this poem, helps me to feel his closeness.

Memory Tree

Today we will plant a tree,
In loving memory,
Around its trunk we will tie,
A ribbon in white to signify,
That love never dies.

Your apple blossoms now bloom each year,
To let us know that you're still here,
In the air, their fragrance sweet,
Reminds us that we will meet,
Once again in Heaven's plan,
With joy untold hand in hand.

Music of the Soul

We cry for ourselves, not loved ones gone,
They are happy in the great beyond,
No more burdens, heartache or stress,
They live in a state of pure happiness.

It's those of us left behind,
Who struggle with the concept of time,
On this planet of pain and tears,
Learning and growing through the years.

What a blessing you were to me,
Like a magnificent symphony,
With haunting passages of turbulent lows,
Mixed with brilliant crescendos.

Across the pages lines of notes play,
But then abruptly go away,
A symphony of the story of you,
My wonderful son of twenty-two.

What movement would be playing now,
If you were still here somehow?
A work of such hope and promise,
With so much more to accomplish.

My darling son,
Your earthly work must have been done,
You are now a more brilliant light,
Just beyond earthly sight.

Composing more passages on another plane,
With knowledge earned through joy and pain,
The music of your soul will always flow,
In our hearts, this we know.

Listening with our inner ear,
The melody is very clear,
We will strive to overcome our sorrow,
In God's promise of a joyous tomorrow.

My Taj Mahal

If it were possible I would build you a Taj Mahal,
A magnificent monument for one and all,
A structure of beauty and inspiration,
To celebrate love for all generations.

My love for you finds expression in poems,
Writing them helps me not feel so alone,
Giving words to the love we share,
Keeps me from giving into despair.

A book of my poetry has come to be,
Words flowing for others to see,
My Taj Mahal on a smaller scale,
A testimony that love never fails.

A gift in celebration of love and life,
Despite loss, anguish, and strife,
You are gone but your light still shines,
Brilliantly glowing for all time.

No Regrets

When your heart is broken,
If words had not been spoken,
Those thoughts would play across your mind,
Sorrow for the waste of time.

So grateful there are no regrets,
For words that were not said,
We spoke most every day,
And my son would always say.

I love you, Mom, and I'd say, I love you too,
Just a natural thing to do,
Take every chance you can,
So your loved ones understand,
The place they hold within your heart,
The anguish if they'd depart.

Wrap your loved ones in your care,
Helping them to be aware,
The gift of family while they're here,
To love and cherish every year.

Rainbow's Promise

A rainbow's arc of spectral light,
What a glorious sight,
Seven colors to be seen,
Orange, yellow, and a lovely green,
Indigo, violet, red and blue,
Radiating with brilliant hues.

Flying through the rainbow,
That's where I want to go,
Following songbirds and happy dreams,
To new heights yet unseen,
No more dark clouds or dreary skies,
Only light and lullabies.

Our teardrops will be gone,
When we go far beyond,
The proverbial pot of gold,
Will be ours to hold,
Among the stars in a dream come true,
Where everything is bright and new.

Seasons

Seasons come and seasons go,
Joy and sorrow we come to know,
Always carried by the tide,
Where do we choose to reside?

Protest, anger, push and pull,
Will we play the part of fool?
Or with dignity and grace,
Handle all we come to face.

Believing there is a plan,
I strive to understand,
All the sorrow and the pain,
We experience on this earthly plane.

Happiness and joy are a part of life too,
I'll never forget the moments we knew,
Remembering our love will help to sustain me,
You live forever in precious memory.

Small Comforts

Two favorite shirts that you wore,
Hang on the back of my closet door,
After you died I hung them there,
To have your scent in the air.

One shirt is plaid, the other tan,
I like to keep them close at hand,
Western style shirts you wore with style,
Now bring a bittersweet smile.

I hold them and wish they were you,
I'd give anything for this to be true,
Inhaling your scent I cry,
Wondering why you had to die.

I talk to you and send hugs and kisses,
To the son this mother sorely misses,
I wish that I could still buy you shirts,
And not have a heart that always hurts.

The buffalo hide boots you loved so much,
Are in our room as well to touch,
Small things of comfort to keep you close,
When I am missing you the most.

Visual reminders of our wonderful boy,
And the years that were filled with so much joy,
I thank God that I was your mother,
And for what we meant to each other.

Step by Step

Love's redeeming grace,
Take away this heartache,
Let me with love and joy recall,
The happy times for us all.

I want to celebrate the love we knew,
For every moment we had with you,
To work through this terrible grief,
With a life now that feels incomplete.

Quiet my cries,
Dry my eyes,
I am so thankful for the time,
I was able to call you mine.

I didn't want this broken heart,
Or to live in a world apart,
This isn't the life I planned,
It's so hard to understand.

I know you want my happiness,
I am doing my best,
As step by step and day by day,
I struggle to find my way.

The Little Things

Notice the little things in life each day,
Gratefully acknowledge and praise,
As your day is about to begin,
Focus on what matters and go within.

Take pleasure in being alive,
We are not meant just to survive,
Smile at the people you see,
Be as pleasant as you can be.

Do you know someone who is sad?
Be thoughtful and help them to feel glad,
Kind words and good deeds,
Mean so much when you're in need.

Be a mentor, be a friend,
Help a broken heart to mend,
Move beyond yourself,
Reach out and be a help.

Thank God for blessings large and small,
With humble acceptance for them all,
In all hardships and terrible pain,
Strive to find the greater gain.

Divine love and spiritual light,
Comfort and keep our spirits bright,
Fill our hearts with joy and love,
With heavenly blessings from above.

The Spark Within

Love never ends,
It moves, it bends,
The spark of light within,
Will always transcend,
Any despair, pain or grief,
Giving the comfort that we seek.

Show me the way,
I pray each day,
Guide me on my journey,
Let there be no hurry,
So that I might rest within my quest,
For love's eternal glory.

Thumbprint of Love

A silver necklace I wear each day,
From your thumb print that was made,
It nestles closely by my heart,
And helps me feel less apart.

The necklace isn't necessary to keep,
A love that is so very deep,
Still, any comfort I can feel,
I gladly take to help me heal.

Engraved on the back, "Love Never Ends,"
Because that's the message that we send,
Until I die the necklace will be,
Worn with love around my neck to see.

When in great joy and delight,
We will once again unite,
Shedding the earthly body I know,
In God's love and heavenly glow.

What to Say

People don't know what to say,
When a loved one passes away,
Keep a stiff upper lip,
What a terrible quip,
No one to blame,
Their life is the same.

They can never truly fathom,
A world without a loved one with them,
And don't even want to think,
How life can change in a blink,
More comfortable to ignore,
They go on as before.

I'm thankful for the people who,
With love and empathy come through,
To help me make it one more day,
When it seems there is no way.

Even in the darkest times,
Spirit somehow seems to find,
A way to impart,
Things to help mend the heart,
A card, a hug, a telephone call,
Things that may seem small,
Mean so much when you wonder when,
You will ever feel whole again.

I am now more aware,
To show others greater care,
So that I might unknowingly,
Lift one up who is in need.

Without Any Warning

As a dedicated mother and wife,
I was very happy with my life,
Busy with my husband, daughter, and son,
I looked forward to things to come.

My entire world changed one morning,
Without any warning,
As I was sleeping in my bed,
I learned my precious son was dead.

How could I imagine to see,
A child of mine die before me?
It goes against the natural order of life,
Leaving us in trauma and strife.

There were times I thought of dying,
Every day I'm still crying,
I can't believe my son is gone,
It's so hard to keep moving on.

Our family of four,
Is no more,
How empty it now feels to me,
To be a family of three.

Sometimes I feel like screaming,
As I search for purpose and meaning,
With the hope that his death will lead,
To something greater to believe.

His life was a gift for whatever the time,
I was blessed to call him mine,
He is gone, and yet he is here,
His presence is felt, warm and dear.

Bodies die but love never ends,
Love is the power that transcends,
He is with me every day,
Only in a different way.

Angelic Gifts and Prayers

❦

The best and most beautiful things in this world cannot be seen or
even heard, but must be felt with the heart.

Helen Keller

An Angel's Kiss

Give your worries, sorrows or fears,
To the angels because they hear,
Feel the heavenly brushing of their wings,
With the divine love that they bring.

I do not want to miss,
The whisper of an angel's kiss,
Or a sign they send to me,
When in faith I believe.

Catch my teardrops when I cry,
I know you watch from on high,
When my pain is too much to bear,
Wrap me in your wings of care.

In the stillness help me find,
The peace that comes from the divine,
And surrender into a sea of love,
Gifts from the angels above.

Angel Boy

My angel boy in Heaven,
Spread your wings and fly,
High amidst the clouds and stars,
Across a twinkling sky.

Another ray of starlight,
Beside a brilliant moon,
Your spirit soars with happiness,
Singing a glorious tune.

A spark of God reunited,
Luminous in your joy,
At home again in Heaven,
My darling angel boy.

Shine your light upon me,
Help me find my way,
The days are filled with shadows,
Since you passed away.

Lead me on to Heaven,
When I die and am reborn,
Sparkling like a diamond,
Where no longer I will mourn.

Two lights that will be shining,
Forever side by side,
With the company of angels,
We'll joyfully abide.

Angel Chimes

I have angel chimes by my front door,
With words that I am hoping for,
Peace and love and serenity,
All the qualities I pray for me.

When the chimes are gently ringing,
I believe angels are bringing,
Healing energies to ground and center,
To everyone that will enter.

How grateful I am to know the divine,
Is surrounding us all the time,
When we open and believe,
There are many gifts that we'll receive.

I welcome in this flow of chi,
With all the positive energy,
So that my house is filled with love,
Blessings from the angels above.

Angel Prayer

Angels and guides be with me each day,
Help me to find my way,
Release any toxins, grief, or stress,
Help me to be my best.

Positive thoughts and affirmations,
No negative vibrations,
Release the sorrow that I feel,
I want my soul to heal.

To live within a state of grace,
Able to handle what I must face,
With divine guidance and intuition,
Bringing forward to fruition.

My life purpose and destination,
Not this sense of desolation,
With the passing of my son,
I don't know how this is done.

Angel wings enfold me now,
With heavenly peace and faith endow,
So that I may find some comfort in,
Living my life once again.

Angelic Arms

Heavenly wings gently enfold,
Cradle me and comfortingly hold,
I cannot live each day in grief,
Rock me softly and bring relief.

Whisper words of joy and peace,
Acceptance and thanks to help and ease,
Songs of love to soothe the soul,
Repairing my heart to make it whole.

Swaying gently in angelic arms,
Safe from all earthly harms,
I will find the strength to take,
All the choices I need to make.

A leap of faith with soul conviction,
Love without any restriction,
Held close, then let go,
With divine assurance to come to know.

We are always surrounded by heavenly care,
Help me to become more aware,
To focus on the gifts through time,
Bestowed upon us by the divine.

Angels Close By

When I hurt and when I cry,
I know my angels are close by,
I refocus and go within,
Receiving strength from Spirit again.

With my inner spiritual ear,
I listen for what I may hear,
Soft little echoes from my soul,
Aiding me in becoming more whole.

With these whispers from inside,
Loving thoughts that help and guide,
I find courage to stand on my own,
Comforted in knowing I'm never alone.

Breathe

Dear God, help me find the peace,
That comes with the sweet release,
Of all resentments, fears or pains,
Anger or judgments where nothing is gained.

These emotions only hurt yourself,
Take a breath, then breathe them out,
Making room inside,
Inviting Spirit to reside.

I want a harmonious living space,
With strength and courage to be able to face,
What each day holds in store for me,
Walking forward confidently.

In happiness, trust and faith,
Surrounded by God's holy grace,
Consciously moving toward the light,
Surrounded by love day and night.

Butterfly

Butterflies are beautiful for us to see,
And come in many varieties,
With brilliant colors and patterned wings,
They bring us joy and make our hearts sing.

On a deeper level they teach us about faith,
And accepting changes that we must make,
The butterfly is the result of transformation,
A new and wonderful creation.

From egg to caterpillar to butterfly,
They break free and take to the sky,
Uplifting messengers of courage and hope,
Especially in times we find it hard to cope.

Lovely symbols of what's possible for us too,
The metamorphosis for me and for you,
Give me courage and faith so that I may soar,
With love and happiness in life once more.

Dragonfly

Dragonflies represent change,
And beside water they like to range,
They also represent our subconscious mind,
And relate to thoughts during meditative times.

A meaningful sign when they appear,
Letting us know our departed ones are near,
Sending us their energy of harmony and peace,
With their beautiful wings to comfort and ease.

I thank the angels each time I see,
A dragonfly circling around me,
It may seem trivial to a few,
But I know they are sent with love by you.

I wrote this with my special friend, Virginia, in mind – she lost her son, too. She has had several unusual dragonfly experiences since her son died. Many people feel that our loved ones in spirit use dragonflies as a sign of their continued love and connection.

Feathers

I often seem to discover,
Different types of feathers,
Small ones, big ones, dark and light,
Somehow come into my sight.

I wonder if they are,
Angelic calling cards,
Messages of comfort and hope,
Helping me to cope.

With angelic breath the feathers have flown,
To let me know that I'm not alone,
With thankfulness and happy tears,
It's wonderful when they appear.

So I take another step,
Realizing that I can't give up,
There is a reason I am here,
The feathers help to make this clear.

Thank you angels for these signs,
I am always grateful when I find,
Another feather for my collection,
Healing wings of love and direction.

After posting this poem on my blog, I went to a local coffee shop. I usually go through the drive-through, but decided to go inside the store this time. As I walked inside the door, I noticed a small white feather on the inside door mat. Ever since my son died, I have been finding a lot of feathers, sometimes in odd places. Feathers can be very symbolic, a bridge between the spirit world and the mortal world, an angelic sign.

Hands Held

My soul is screaming,
I am clawing at the door,
Please God, I know there is more,
What am I here for?

Remove the veils,
My spirit wails,
I want to be with my son,
I can't lose our connection.

A life, a love, a joy divine,
Gone, what I thought was mine,
Hands held, faces kissed,
Oh God, so dearly missed.

Only borrowed, never owned,
Love, the pattern sown,
A kiss, a hug, a tender sigh,
I will never say goodbye.

So many questions – why, God, why?
Will I have no answers until I die?
Help me to find what I seek,
Open my heart and give relief.

A hand held, yet released,
A heart, that can be at peace.

Healing Prayer

In my deepest despair,
I turned to the Lord's Prayer,
And now every day,
I contemplate the words I say.

When my son died,
It made me realize,
That there must be so much more,
Than what I thought I came here for.

Otherwise life would make no sense,
What would be the defense,
Against this hopelessness and grief?
There would be no relief.

Show me God, what my purpose is,
For I don't want to live,
With emptiness and questions why,
Reveal to me what I ache to know,
To help my spirit heal and grow.

Hummingbird

Tiny hummingbird flying by,
A flash of color in the sky,
With the blurred beating of your little wings,
What is the message that you bring?

The beauty in life is what you remind us of,
And to appreciate the things we love,
To move forward, not looking back,
So we don't focus on what we lack.

You also help us to feel joy inside,
Gratitude for being alive,
To savor each moment and to open our hearts,
Searching for the sweetness that life can impart.

What a beautiful winged messenger to see,
With wonderful symbology,
Thank you hummingbird, for showing us the way,
To find happiness in each new day.

Miracles

Miracles do happen, I can see,
Because you are now communicating with me,
This connection I've yearned for deep in my soul,
Has been my most fervent goal.

Knowing we can connect from different spheres,
Is profoundly comforting when you're not here,
I could not bear the loss of the closeness we knew,
What a gift to have you come through.

How healing to know that all is one,
On this journey I've begun,
I am working on what I can learn,
As my life takes this new turn.

What a blessing that you stay near,
Helping to make my path more clear,
Without this reassurance from the divine,
It would be easy to give up over time.

I pray my suffering and sorrow will transform,
Into peace and joy as hope is reborn,
Love is the message and the call,
For it is love that sustains us all.

Thank you for being a messenger from Spirit,
With God's grace I am able to hear it,
This validation that love never ends,
Helps give me the faith that my heart will mend.

Now I Lay Me Down to Sleep

Now I lay me down to sleep,
I pray that I will find relief,
It's too hard to live each day in grief,
Please God, help me find your peace.

It's not easy living each day,
Now that my son has passed away,
A conflict because I feel him near,
Though physically he's not here.

Maybe tonight I will see,
My son alive in a dream with me,
A glimpse back to our lives before,
He walked through Heaven's door.

Or, perhaps unknowingly,
I am with him when I sleep,
Traveling with him to a different realm,
Where God's joy and peace abound.

To find the bridge between his world and mine,
Is what I seek to find,
Take my hand and lead me there,
Help me to be more aware.

To know that separation isn't true,
That I will always be one with you,
And with God's love and divine help,
I will realize my greater self.

On My Knees

Brought to my knees,
With agonizing need,
When the world without,
Turned to darkness and doubt,

No place to hide,
I went inside,
Desperate for my pain to ease,
And for faith in which to believe.

I prayed to God,
I cried so hard,
Why is my child dead?
It should be me instead.

With God's love and Heavenly help,
Move me beyond thoughts of self,
To see the greater picture and plan,
So I might come to understand.

Let me feel your divine love,
With all comfort from above,
To replace my anguish and grief,
With the peace that I seek.

Phone Calls from Heaven

When the kitchen phone lights up in its base,
You can see the joy on my face,
When I see the screen turn blue,
I know it's you coming through.

It's one of your signs that I love most of all,
Because I miss your telephone calls,
Thank you for checking in to say,
Hi mom, I didn't really go away.

I still want you to know,
That I will always love you so,
And I am forever by your side,
Let my love be your guide.

It's not the same, but I'm still here,
Feel my presence ever near,
With the love that we knew,
Know that I am still calling you.

Prayers and Meditations

I ask you, God, for your gift of peace,
Take away my hopelessness and grief,
Guide me to the answers I seek,
So in Spirit's arms I'll find relief.

Surround me in your heavenly embrace,
Comfort and support to help me face,
A future now unknown to me,
Not what I'd thought it would be.

Hear my prayers and meditations,
Take away all hesitations,
For a heart that is shattered and broken,
Send your love to heal and open.

I don't want to live in fear,
Now that my son's not physically here,
Or live each day in a degree of depression,
Wondering if this pain will lessen.

Life is hard, I can't do it by myself,
Thank you for any heavenly help,
With God's grace and divine inspiration,
I pray for spiritual transformation.

Rainbow From Heaven

Thank you for the rainbow you gave us to see,
Beside your blossoming apple tree,
What a beautiful symbol of,
Your continuous presence and love.

The colors were pure and bright,
In the afternoon light,
Violet and yellow, green and blue,
A gift of spirit given by you.

Tears were running down my face,
It was almost like feeling your embrace,
I miss you being physically here,
Your human form so warm and dear.

It helps when I am feeling low,
To think about your lovely rainbow,
A bridge between your world and mine,
Another one of your heavenly signs.

With a heart broken open,
In God's devotion,
We'll move beyond preconceived notions,
Limiting views and human emotions.

Because there is no greater bond than love,
It's what the universe is made of,
And with the knowledge that all is one,
There is no separation, my precious son.

Signs From Above

Synchronicities, electricity,
Songs, messages, and feathers,
Clocks, numbers, license plates,
And letters that tell of forever.

You were with me once, and with me now,
In many ways you tell me how,
Thank you for your loving presence,
We still have your eternal essence.

On days when I feel I stumble,
Your love keeps me ever humble,
Unceasingly, you try to show,
The way in which I should go.

Thank you son, angels and guides,
With new vision clear my eyes,
Fill my soul with joy and love,
With divine inspiration from above.

What Must Be

Dear God, I am on my knees,
Praying for this pain to cease,
What have I come here for?
My life is not as it was before.

Must we suffer in order to grow?
Is this the only way we can know,
The spirit that dwells within,
Our temporary earthly skin?

Fill the emptiness that is inside,
Walk with me by my side,
I cannot do this by myself,
I ask for all heavenly help.

Enfold me in your arms of grace,
With divine love to replace,
The grief and sadness that live in me,
With acceptance of what must be.

Winged Messengers

Dragonflies, butterflies, hummingbirds and crows,
Through many winged things you help us to know,
That you are still here with us,
And that we must,
See life in a deeper way,
To be able to recognize the signs that say,
I love you mother, I love you dad,
I don't want you to be so sad.

I surround you with my love and care,
Look and be aware,
My body died, but that wasn't me,
I am still here for you to see,
I want you to heal and to feel,
The connection that will always be,
Between you and me.

I am trying my best,
So that you might rest,
And understand, this is part of a divine plan,
To come to know that it was my time to go,
That each of us gains a rest,
When we pass our life's tests.

I am waiting for you until your work is done,
When we'll be together again as one,
Until that time I watch and guide,
With love from the other side.

Celebrations of Life

❧

Celebrate love. It is the breath of your existence
and the best of all reasons for living.

Author Unknown

A Birthday Candle

This morning we light a candle,
And watch the flame at play,
A candle lit with all our love,
On this special day.

Gone, but not forgotten,
Forever in our hearts,
The candle flame reminds us,
We are never far apart.

A life and love remembered,
We honor you this day,
And celebrate our moments,
Time can never take away.

For each precious memory,
For every treasured year,
We are so very grateful,
For the time that you were here.

Happy birthday to you in Heaven,
Feel the wishes that we send,
We'll be your mom and dad forever,
Our love will never end.

A Birthday That Won't Be

Twenty-five years ago today,
Was our son's birthday,
The thirtieth of March in 1985,
Was the special day that he arrived.

What a day of wondrous joy,
To give birth to our precious boy,
We had a daughter and now a son,
What a feeling of perfection.

Almost three years ago our son passed away,
On a beautiful September day,
The moon was full, the stars were bright,
As he was walking, enjoying the night.

A freak accident, in seconds he was dead,
What words can ever be said?
Twenty-two years full of adventure and life,
Were suddenly gone, as if cut with a knife.

All the years of love and devotion,
Disappeared, like the tides in an ocean,
I am left floundering on the shore,
Wondering what I am here for.

Searching for answers, searching for peace,
Praying at some point this pain will cease,
Remembering a birthday that won't be,
Is still unbelievable to me.

A Christmas Wreath

This will be the third December,
We will place a wreath and remember,
Every Christmas memory of our son,
From his birth until age twenty-one.

An evergreen wreath with a red velvet bow,
A symbolic sign on his grave to show,
Undying love and gratitude for,
The son we will miss forever more.

A New Year

In 2007 you went to heaven,
Now it is 2009,
Where is the time?
I cried when the new year came,
For nothing was the same,
Without you here it felt so wrong,
To have time move along.

There was the fear,
That with each new year,
Your memory might fade,
Taking us further away,
Crazy, I know, because where could you go?
You are always here with me,
In every single breath I breathe.

It doesn't matter how much time passes,
Or what year it is,
Because love never disappears,
So march on, time, you can never erase,
The cherished moments forever embraced,
Deeply embedded within our hearts,
Neither time nor distance can ever part.

A Year of Firsts

The first year after you died,
I was just trying to survive,
Every day felt like a week,
I was overwhelmed by grief.

Trying to make it through each first,
Was beyond imagining in its hurt,
The first Thanksgiving without you here,
Was the first holiday we had to fear.

Your dad's birthday came next,
So empty without you to expect,
You always added so much fun,
What a joy to have had our son.

Then it was Christmas when you were sorely missed,
I never thought I'd have to endure this,
My favorite family time of celebration,
Will never be the same occasion.

I could not send a card to you,
On Valentine's Day like I used to do,
No more cards to sons about love,
Or candy treats you were fond of.

In March you would have been twenty-three,
But it was never meant to be,
No more birthdays to share with you,
Memories will have to carry us through.

Easter was the next special day,
And it was not observed in the same way,
It was a more quiet time of reflection,
With deeper thoughts about Christ's resurrection.

My birthday was in April and I missed you so,
The pain was more than I could know,
Without you here to share the day,
Was sadder than I can ever say.

Mother's Day was bittersweet,
I felt so incomplete,
Last Mother's Day you had spent with me,
And all of the family.

The following month was June,
In which Father's Day came too soon,
No longer here to share with your dad,
How could we not feel bad?

We had no Fourth of July picnic that year,
Like we did when you were near,
No get together of food and fun,
It wouldn't have been the same without our son.

The most difficult first was in September,
The month you died and we'll always remember,
An anniversary we never imagined,
Inconceivable that this happened.

Somehow a year passed by,
Without a day I didn't cry,
No more firsts to face with dread,
Screams of why inside my head.

On special occasions we set your place,
And on your birthday we have a cake,
We light a candle for you each night,
To hold you close in eternal light.

Two years now have passed,
Since we saw you last,
I still cry every day,
The pain never goes away.

It's not as piercing of an ache,
But my heart still breaks,
I'm learning to live each day as it comes,
To find some peace with each setting sun.

The future is never ours to know,
Cherish every moment and learn and grow,
I work to focus on what was gained,
To remember the love and joy, not the pain.

Angels Across the USA

Angels across the USA,
Are our children who passed away,
Flying now with angelic wings,
Accompanying Alan as he sings.

Songs of hope and songs of faith,
Songs of love and heartbreak,
Our children are the chorus we hear,
Their voices blending strong and clear.

We love you angel daughters and sons,
Bring your message to everyone,
Love is eternal, love never dies,
Together forever, no final good-byes.

I wrote this poem after the evening we heard Alan Pedersen perform and speak at an event sponsored by our local Bereaved Parents of the USA chapter. Alan is a gifted singer/songwriter/speaker who lost his daughter in 2001. Through this grief and trauma he has focused his talents on comforting the bereaved. As of the date of publication of this book he has produced three beautiful CD's dealing with the loss of a child.

During 2010 Alan and his wife are driving across the country bringing his healing message to grieving families. The tour is called Angels Across the USA, and its purpose is to increase awareness of grief organizations that reach out to bereaved families. Our son is one of the angels traveling with him. There is a link to his wonderful work in the Helpful Resources section at the back of the book. Bless Alan and his wife Denise in their inspired journey.

Balloons of Love

Today under a clear blue sky,
Wiping tears from our eyes,
We will release our balloons,
Commemorating lives gone too soon.

On wings of love we set them free,
For our angel children to see,
Floating through space and time,
Past the staircase we wish we could climb.

A symbolic gesture that helps us heal,
From the sorrow that we feel,
Another means for us to say,
They live in our hearts every day.

Balloons filled with laughter, balloons filled with tears,
Balloons filled with memories for the time they were here,
Dancing in the sunlight on currents of air,
Brimming with thanks for all that we shared.

We imagine our children on the other side,
Catching the balloons as they glide,
Red and yellow, purple and gold,
They know which balloon is theirs to hold.

We know they are happy, they are dancing now too,
And we want to celebrate all that we knew,
Forever our daughters, forever our sons,
Only temporarily parted, our precious ones.

We attended the Bereaved Parents of the USA Northern Virginia Chapter's third annual Memory Walk, Picnic, and Balloon Release in the spring of 2010. It was a very meaningful event. There is a connection that goes beyond words between bereaved parents. I read three of my poems as part of the program before the balloon release, including this one, which I wrote for the occasion. We will always celebrate our children's lives and love! There is a link to the Bereaved Parents national website in the Helpful Resources section at the back of the book.

Christmas Sorrow and Joy

Christmas was only three months after you died,
I don't know how I survived,
The thought of no presents for you under the tree,
Emotionally brought me to my knees.

I had artwork framed that you had done,
Beautiful images from our son,
And ordered an afghan with your picture and a poem,
To wrap up in while I'm at home.

I found ornaments for you with special meaning,
Lovely angels and bright stars gleaming,
Memorial items for the house,
To feel your presence all about.

I was still Christmas shopping for you,
Without consciously meaning to,
Finding some comfort for the anguish within,
Working desperately not to give in.

Two years later I am making progress,
For you I can do no less,
Working hard to accept each day,
And to understand my life this way.

Change is inevitable, that is true,
But how could I expect losing you?
I have to accept what I cannot change,
Because life will never be the same.

Love is the constant to depend on,
Whether in this world or beyond,
The physical body dies,
But love survives.

So, as the holidays draw near again,
Feel the love to you I send,
With my blessing of gratitude and cheer,
For the time that you were here.

Eternal Valentine

A gift of love that transcends time,
The perfect Valentine,
Thank you for the words that flow,
The love that just seems to grow,
The reassurance to know,
That we are never truly apart,
But heart to heart,
Forever entwined,
My eternal Valentine.

I wrote my first poem ("Only Son") on February 12, 2009, and wrote this one shortly afterward. I think now that the timing of these poems was significant because they came to me around Valentine's Day, a holiday that celebrates love. What better timing could there have been for the gift of these poems, which are centered around the eternal nature of love.

Family Christmas Tree

There are many special ornaments to see,
Upon our beautiful Christmas tree,
Brought with love from far and near,
They tell our story from year to year.

Our first Christmas together was 1980,
The year that we were married,
We became proud parents in 1982,
When our lovely daughter joined us two.

Three years later our son was born,
On a March Korean morn,
In the Army while stationed overseas,
Was where our son joined us three.

Major milestones in our life,
Once we became husband and wife,
With ornaments to mark these occasions,
In happiness and celebration.

A red and gold angel is on top of the tree,
Gazing out in serenity,
A celestial guardian of all we hold dear,
As we decorate the tree each year.

There are angels and stars,
Saxophones and guitars,
Musical instruments our children played,
On the branches all arrayed.

Old fashioned Santas and Sheltie ornaments too,
Bells and birds to name a few,
Soldiers and trains, snowmen and dolls,
With red and gold poinsettias surrounding them all.

A Christmas tree that tells a story,
Of love and family in all its glory,
Sadly, there is also pain,
For we will not see our son again.

Two years ago he suddenly died,
Leaving us to wonder why,
Memorial ornaments now also adorn our tree,
Keeping our son close in loving memory.

A tree of love, a tree of hope,
A tree of sadness and of ways to cope,
Within its branches a tale to tell,
Of a family who loved long and well.

Forever Our Son

It's the second September since you passed away,
The second anniversary to visit your grave,
Your dad and I stood there in disbelief,
To lose our son and be in grief.

We placed a bouquet of flowers, red and gold,
Vibrant fall colors to behold,
Above the gravestone with your name,
And contemplated how our lives have changed.

One day your dad and I,
Will be lying by your side,
One gravestone sharing our last name,
A family linked together again.

Gravestones are the visible signs,
Of lives lived through time,
But it is in dying that we are reborn,
Returning to spirit form.

Physically now separated, that is true,
But we are never apart from you,
Forever you will be our son,
Eternally linked in love as one.

Holidays

The holidays are a particularly poignant time of year,
With friends and family gathering near,
We have fond memories of holidays past,
Amazed the years go by so fast.

In our minds a movie plays,
Of the many wonderful holidays,
We smell the turkey and taste the pies,
And sip hot apple cider with happy sighs.

Sometimes we travel, sometimes stay home,
So very fortunate if we're not alone,
Good spirits and laughter fill the air,
With hugs and sharing everywhere.

Catching up on the latest news,
Remembering old family stories too,
It's these special memories that remain in our hearts,
Softening the pain when loved ones depart.

Cook up a feast and say a prayer,
For our many blessings and be aware,
Cherish each moment and give praise,
For the blessing that love brings to our days.

My Birthday

The day has dawned bright and clear,
Another birthday without you here,
I am doing better this year than last,
With the three years that have passed.

I still see you with me back then,
Home with us for the celebration,
You watched as I put candles on my cake,
The one which I had happily baked.

I have a great picture of you and me,
It is a wonderful memory,
A mother and son sharing a special day,
Never imagining you would pass away.

I don't like to see pictures of me now,
My face is not the same somehow,
I look a little sad and drawn,
Ever since you've been gone.

Maybe one day a spark of life will return,
As I continue to live and learn,
There will be no happily ever after,
But I have the memories of love and laughter.

Nativity

When the holidays were over this year,
Putting away the nativity set brought tears,
Mary knows what I am going through,
She lost her son, too,
I asked for her compassion, mercy, and grace,
As the tears ran down my face.

I pray for all heavenly help,
Knowing I can't recover by myself,
Believing that many spiritual helpers guide,
Lovingly from the other side,
I work to open to their gifts,
So I may feel my soul uplift.

Through this unimaginable pain,
Every day I strive to gain,
The faith that only Heaven can send,
To help this sorrow to transcend,
To rise beyond my profound grief,
So that I may find the peace I seek.

eflections of Love

ions of love, visions of hope,
theme to help parents to cope,
ther in shared heartache and loss,
by the enormity of the cost.

are gone, our hearts are broken,
ords can ever be spoken?
ath in a world now unknown,
know we need not walk alone.

ssionate friends all carrying grief,
Driven to heal and to find some relief,
Searching for hope in our lives once more,
Because they will never be as they were before.

Joining hands with each other,
We reflect and remember,
The ties of the heart with our children,
Grateful for the gift we were given.

It is in love that we will survive,
Love that keeps our sons and daughters alive,
Our children never really leave,
They are with us in every breath we breathe.

The theme for the Compassionate Friends' Thirty-Third National Conference was "reflections of love, visions of hope." I wrote this poem with this theme in mind. The Compassionate Friends is a national organization with local chapters across the country, providing support for parents and other relatives following the death of a child (regardless of age). There is a link to their website in the Helpful Resources section at the back of the book.

Thanksgiving

On Thanksgiving day we will say a prayer,
With family and friends gathered there,
Thankful all to be together,
Sharing the holiday with each other.

There will be a place set at the table for you,
Knowing you will be joining us too,
Looking down from Heaven above,
Surrounding us with your love.

Your physical absence will be keenly felt,
But your spiritual presence will be felt throughout,
You never missed a holiday while you were here,
Death won't keep you from being near.

Happy Thanksgiving, dearest one,
We are so blessed you were our son,
We thank God for the gift of you,
And remember you in all we do.

Thanksgiving Without You

It's a dreary, rainy, cloudy day,
Everything is draped in gray,
The weather matches perfectly,
The melancholy blanketing me.

Three days from now will be Thanksgiving,
I never imagined you'd not be living,
Children shouldn't die before their parents do,
It's so hard to believe this is true.

Every day I pray for help,
To understand what this is about,
You are in your heavenly home,
And I feel so alone.

When we eat our pumpkin pie,
I will try not to cry,
It's the one I would make for you,
You always enjoyed a slice or two.

It's the little things that are bittersweet,
All the moments that make our lives complete,
Memories pieced together,
That stay with us forever.

There are smiles and there are tears,
For every single precious year,
I love you, Graham, I miss you so,
More than anyone could ever know.

The Thirtieth of March

We are having a birthday party for you this year,
Your good friends will all be here,
Twenty-four years old you would be today,
Had you not passed away.

There will be lots of food that I will make,
And your handsome face is on the cake,
Birthday candles, plates and napkins,
It's still so hard to believe this happened.

In our backyard,
Where your apple trees are,
We will release balloons,
Commemorating a life gone too soon.

With messages of remembrance and love,
To float to you in the sky above,
The day will be bittersweet,
Mixed feelings of joy and grief.

Joy for every moment we shared,
Love that was beyond compare,
Sorrow that our time together is gone,
We must now look beyond.

Certain you will join us in spirit,
This will surely help to cheer us,
As we celebrate a life well lived,
With all the love that we can give.

This picture is from 2009 when we had Graham's closest friends over to celebrate his birthday. The day was much easier with them here. It was wonderful to reminisce about the good times they all had together. We are very thankful that Graham had such good friends. Their love for Graham and continued ties with us mean so much. Thank you Julia, Mike, Vineet, and Jack.

Worldwide Candle Lighting

All of our lost children, young and old,
We gather now and gently hold,
Remembering with our every breath,
That love never ends, not even in death.

A heartbroken group of fathers and mothers,
With a sorrow unimaginable to others,
Struggling to overcome the most devastating blow,
Bonded in grief we never thought to know.

With each candle that we light,
We feel our children's spirits burning bright,
Every beloved child's face we see,
Forever in our memory.

In the candles' golden glow,
Even though our tears still flow,
We cherish every moment we had with you,
Though the days were far too few.

We love you now, we'll love you forever,
As your parents we will always treasure,
The blessing of our daughters and sons,
Our dearly loved, precious ones.

The Compassionate Friends, a national organization for grieving families, holds a Worldwide Candle Lighting every December in memory of our lost children. I wrote this poem and read it at my local Chapter's observance. There is a link to the Compassionate Friends' website in the Helpful Resources section at the back of the book.

Songs of the Spirit

❦

{T}he spirit giveth life.

2 Corinthians 3:6 (King James Version)

A Master Plan

Do you believe in magic,
And that it can happen from something tragic,
That from the deepest misery,
We may gain a great victory?

Do you believe that our earthly skin,
Is only the vessel for our spirit within,
That our true self is not what we see,
And that we are a part of eternity?

The here and now is not the whole,
In the journey of a soul,
But it's hard to have the comprehension,
For soul contracts and multi-dimensions.

When we come here without conscious knowledge,
Of what our souls want to accomplish,
And when we experience heartache, death, and loss,
It's natural to question the cost.

We ask for answers from the universe,
When times are at their worst,
And yet we must ultimately trust,
That life will prove to be just.

If we surrender our will,
And listen and be still,
We may hear our spirit song,
Knowing we are where we belong.

I don't want to live a lukewarm life,
Trampled down from all the strife,
No big highs and no big lows,
Everything just the status quo.

Hopefully the day will come,
When once more I'll want to run,
To laugh and play in the rain,
No longer carrying so much pain.

A worthy goal to pursue,
Something I must work to do,
Free of regrets for what has passed,
Because there is only one thing that ever lasts.

That is love, and that I knew,
It will help to see me through,
Help me focus on my life's gifts,
That in joy my soul may lift.

Let me be comforted and reassured,
That everything that we endure,
Has the touch of a Master hand,
And is all a part of a divine plan.

A Spiritual Quest

I yearn, I burn to reunite,
With what temporarily is not in sight,
Although uncertain where to go,
It's a journey I must know.

Compelled to take to flight,
Trusting my soul will alight,
I venture on a spiritual quest,
Toward my soul's eternal rest.

The path is hard and travel-worn,
With many hearts broken and torn,
Take my hand and help me to fly,
Triumphantly into the sky.

Open my eyes so that I may see,
All the potential that lies within me,
To rise above all earthly pain,
Transforming with heavenly gain.

Acceptance

I pray for my heart to be open, my focus clear,
To reveal to me why I am here,
To help me focus on the now,
Releasing the past and future somehow.

Fully living all days as they come,
Knowing they are part of the sum,
I don't want to look back with regret,
On expectations that were unmet.

Thankful for opportunities to love and grow,
Accepting all happiness and sorrow,
Believing that all is as it should be,
Please grant me this serenity.

Love that was is never lost,
Love is worth whatever its cost,
A gift to honor and to treasure,
Comforted in knowing that love is forever.

Across Dimensions

If mediums can talk to you,
I should be able to,
No one could be closer,
To you than your mother.

I long to consciously communicate,
No matter how long it will take,
I am working hard each day,
Searching to find the way.

If everything is energy,
Vibrating at different frequencies,
I know it's possible to tune in,
The secret is to go within.

I now see the world with different eyes,
There is so much more to realize,
The here and now is much too small,
To ever be able to explain it all.

To see, touch, hear, taste, and smell,
Are all very well,
But there are other senses to uncover,
Intuition and psychic abilities to discover.

Looking for messages and signs,
Tuning in to the divine,
I know you watch and wait for me,
Until I am able to see.

What has always been right here,
When we move beyond our fear,
I am coming, it won't be long,
The bond of love is much too strong.

To ever keep us far apart,
Because you beat within my heart,
Two hands reaching across dimensions,
With love and joy beyond comprehension.

Always Near

Every day I feel you near,
Your spirit and energy are still here,
Because I don't see you physically,
Doesn't mean you cease to be.

In my life you will always stay,
Nothing can take your presence away,
Grateful for every moment we had together,
Comforted in knowing our love is forever.

I work to not dwell in the past,
Because the blessing of you will forever last,
To bring that forward to the now,
Is what I strive to accomplish somehow.

I am doing the best that I can,
I pray that Spirit understands,
The mourning process is long and slow,
My child's death not a grief I thought to know.

So many emotions to process and release,
On the road to finding peace,
Thank you for the signs you've shown,
To help me not feel so alone.

Knowing you are part of a divine team,
Always present, but not necessarily seen,
Gives me strength to journey on,
When I feel all joy is gone.

Bless you angels, bless you guides,
Thank you loved ones on the other side,
I feel the support and love from you,
With the deepest gratitude.

Heavenly solace for soul-deep pain,
Divine love for me to gain,
Open my heart so that I may receive,
The gift of grace to heal and believe.

Awaken

When our mind is clear,
We may hear,
That still small voice,
That gives us choice.

Awaken the sleeping me,
From the dream we think we see,
And with more open eyes,
To see beyond the outer guise.

Clear my mind of all the chatter,
Let me focus on what matters,
Love, compassion, unity,
Patience, tolerance, and empathy.

Kindness for my fellow man,
Responsibility to lend a hand,
Intuition to follow and know,
The way in which I should go.

Wisdom in picking which battles to fight,
Striving always to be a light,
Join my hand and let us see,
All that we have come here to be.

Beyond the Veil

How wonderful it must be,
To return to pure energy,
Unencumbered, happy and free,
Having shed the earthly body.

No more physical aches or pains,
Heartache, resentments or emotional strains,
Only love and joy prevail,
When we move beyond the veil.

Reconnected to our source and shown,
All the answers we longed to have known,
Beyond the ego and multi-dimensional,
Able to see our greatest potential.

While in the body here on earth,
Experiencing the years from our birth,
It's hard to see past the illusion and live,
With the greater wisdom that is God's to give.

Open my heart and my mind,
So while I'm here I may find,
Strength from Spirit to understand,
My soul's purpose in the divine plan.

Connected

When one person heals, so does another,
Because energy travels to others,
We realize we are all connected,
Linked in ways perhaps unexpected.

Conscious of our thoughts and actions,
Be responsible for things that happen,
There is power in intentions,
Let love lay the foundations.

Like a ripple in a pond,
The effects expand beyond,
So in conscious unity,
We help uplift humanity.

As we contribute to the world,
Our spiritual gifts will unfurl,
And we will write a new story,
For mankind's eternal glory.

Contemplations

Sometimes I think I should be,
Living in a nunnery,
Its name "Our Lady of Perpetual Sorrows,"
Because that's how I see my tomorrows.

Endless days of pain and grief,
Hard to imagine any relief,
As day after day dawns,
I don't know how I manage to go on.

Ever since you died,
I have cried,
So devastated by this all,
The tears continuously fall.

Thoughts of a life of contemplation,
If it could bring some consolation,
Has a certain appeal,
When life feels so unreal.

But I have other family that need me,
So I am working not to be,
Bound by chains of heartache,
For all of our sakes.

We don't have to live in isolation,
To find some consolation,
And I think we must reach out,
To others that need help.

As time moves along,
I gradually feel more strong,
Despite the fear of wondering when,
It will be possible to feel happy again.

And that somehow if I do,
It will diminish the importance of you,
A mother doesn't want to let go,
It goes against every instinct she knows.

But in mourning if we open to hope,
Somehow managing to cope,
By surrendering what we want to keep,
We can find that which we seek.

Healing for our broken hearts,
Comfort to know we are never truly apart,
With Spirit appearing as a dove,
Bringing the gift of eternal love.

Dance With the Divine

I want to dance with life's melody,
In perfect joy and harmony,
No discordant notes to hear,
Just lovely music in my ear.

With the rhythm I will flow,
Twirling and bending as I go,
Gracefully moving, in perfect accord,
With the steps I came here for.

In attunement with the divine,
Aware that everything is by design,
The strains of love will always play,
To gently lift my cares away.

Faith

The Bible says that all you need,
Is faith the size of a mustard seed,
I pray that this is true,
Because it's so hard living without you.

I just want you to come home,
Every day I feel so alone,
I can't believe that you are dead,
Why isn't it me instead?

How is this supposed to be,
That my son would die before me?
I don't want to be wondering why,
Heartbroken until I die.

Build me up with faith anew,
With divine love to see me through,
The darkness in which I now live,
To the light that is God's to give.

Faith and Trust

I want to be in the flow,
Learning daily as I go,
Don't let me miss the signs,
Being sent by the divine.

An unexamined life would be a waste,
We are here to grow and embrace,
Relationships and soul lessons,
Life's trials and tribulations.

Overcoming adversity and pain,
Striving for the greater gain,
Always evolving, don't let me fall,
I am working on understanding it all.

Fill my soul with faith and trust,
Secure in facing what I must,
Surrounded always by heavenly hosts,
Father, Son, and Holy Ghost.

Go Within

Go within for what you seek,
Hear your soul softly speak,
Quieting your mind,
And you will find,
Help in dealing with what must be,
Inner peace and serenity.

Give your anguish up to God,
Some things are just too hard,
Surrender and let go,
Tap into the divine flow,
Learning to accept with grace,
All in life that we may face.

Homecoming

When we cross over after we die,
There's a celebration on the other side,
Do not cry when earthly life is done,
We are back home, moving to a higher rung.

The soul is eternal, we never end,
And we will all be together again,
Our loved ones cheer our return,
Rejoicing with us in what we have learned.

Our concept of time is limited while here,
We only think it's linear,
There is no measurement for time,
In the universe's eternal rhyme.

Give me the enlightenment to see,
That all is as it's meant to be,
Time seems to move too fast or too slow,
But with a spiritual perspective we come to know.

That whether life is short or long,
We are where we belong,
Playing out the plans of our soul,
On the path to becoming whole.

Into the Light

Life has many mysteries I long to have revealed,
Teachings and truths that seem concealed,
Traveling through time we gradually see,
What we thought was hidden is waiting to be freed.

It's our vision that changes,
When perception rearranges,
For when we start to awaken,
Old thoughts and views are shaken.

Mysteries suddenly become more clear,
When we listen with a divine ear,
We learn the greatest teaching hides in plain sight,
Love is what brings us all to the Light.

Live From the Heart

Be in the world, but not of it, I have heard the phrase,
It's now how I live my days,
Shakespeare had it right when he wrote,
"All the world's a stage," to quote.

Since you died my perception has changed,
I no longer live life in close range,
Now I stand somewhat apart,
But strive to live from my heart.

Viewing life from a distance,
Praying for heavenly assistance,
Surrendering into the flow,
I am learning to let go.

All things are possible with divine love and aid,
Understanding and acceptance for the plan that was laid,
My heart is broken but I am trying my best,
To mend and recover from this grievous test.

No one fully understands the bond that we had,
Or why under the surface I always am sad,
There is never a minute that you are not missed,
My wonderful son and most treasured wish.

I loved you on earth and I love you in Heaven,
Love crosses all dimensions,
The ties of the heart are eternal and strong,
Connected forever within love's bond.

Lotus

From the murky depths of mud and debris,
The lotus grows upward striving to break free,
A beautiful flower growing under water,
Surfaces and delights one with its power.

Lovely soft petals that gently unfold,
Simple and elegant to behold,
A dormant seed that bursts into life,
Symbolizing the journey of a soul into light.

Everything in its time is the message to see,
Divine timing playing out beautifully,
No force or impatience to hurry and grow,
Towards the enlightenment of the soul.

Love

Love, unconditional,
The guiding principle,
When all else fails,
Love will prevail.

The greatest power there is to know,
When we tap into its flow,
A universal energy from God,
Strength for us when life is hard.

Accept, surrender, be at peace,
Open your heart and release,
As spirit having a human life,
Distance yourself from earthly strife.

Through the filter of love's eyes,
We can become very wise,
When we focus and search within,
Transformation will begin.

God provides so we don't fail,
Through life's trials and travails,
With unconditional support and love,
We learn what we are capable of.

In thankfulness and praise,
Acknowledge Spirit's ways,
Be a channel of love and goodwill,
To help uplift the world and heal.

Love Unlocks the Door

How unreal and pointless life seems,
When death takes away your dreams,
There are no words to express,
The feelings of hopelessness.

It's not that you value others less,
But life loses a lot of its zest,
When your loved one will no longer be,
In this world for you to see.

The picture now feels so incomplete,
Without my son's presence sweet,
Hard enough when a life was long,
But my child's death just seems so wrong.

My heart aches,
I live in heartbreak,
Without him here there is far less pleasure,
Only his memories to treasure.

I am working hard every day,
To feel joy again come my way,
Not wanting to focus on the pain,
Only the love from him we gained.

Life never stays the same,
It is all about change,
In the times we think we can't bear,
We can become more aware.

We move beyond our physical ties,
Seeing with our spiritual eyes,
That there must be a bigger plan,
To strive to understand.

The eternal truth and master key,
Is really not a mystery,
It is love that unlocks the door,
To what we are searching for.

I want to soar above,
Filled with faith and God's love,
And in grace be transformed,
With joy and purpose reborn.

Mysteries Inside of Me

If all life's answers are within,
Then that's where I'll begin,
I don't have to travel far,
To look for things that already are.

Mysteries inside of me,
Waiting patiently to be,
Unwrapped, examined, and revealed,
No longer to be concealed.

Trust and faith and intuition,
May God's love bring to fruition,
Acceptance, wisdom, and strength of being,
Confidence in the all-seeing.

To bring joy and peace of mind,
That I am working hard to find,
Knowing that death is not the end,
Just a change of form again.

As above, so below,
There is a universal flow,
I want to know why I am here,
And not live my life in fear.

Looking forward to the day,
When my life has played,
So in contentment I'll be at rest,
Knowing while here I did my best.

Never Alone

Guide me each day to live from the heart,
From the moment my day starts,
Let me be a channel of love,
Flowing with guidance from Heaven above.

By focusing on Spirit from within,
Intuitively I'll know where to begin,
No judgments, no impatience, no worry or strife,
As I learn to accept all in my life.

Living in synchronicity and flow,
Confidently walking to where I will go,
The faith that I am never alone,
Strengthens me as I journey Home.

Never Apart

Your dad and I are flying to Germany today,
To tour and visit friends along the way,
It's emotional as I wait to fly,
Because it feels as if I'm saying good-bye.

It's been two years since you died,
But when I'm home you feel close by,
I didn't know that venturing so far from home,
Could make me feel more alone.

It's not a rational way to feel,
You are with me always as I heal,
I feel your love surrounding me,
Like a hug I cannot see.

I wish that as the flight ascends,
I could visit you in Heaven,
Or touch you on a shining star,
Instead of gazing upward from afar.

Fanciful concepts that are not true,
But lovely imaginings as I think of you,
You are actually very near,
Living in a different sphere.

Help me to enjoy this vacation,
And think of you in celebration,
Because we are never really apart,
You are with me in every beat of my heart.

In September 2009 my husband and I flew to Germany for a two week vacation. It had been exactly two years since Graham died, and this trip was the first time since then that I was away from home more than overnight. I didn't realize that being gone from home for a longer time would be so emotional until I was sitting on the plane. While waiting to take off, I began to cry. I started writing this poem while trying to understand why I was so upset. Later, I realized that we get into routines that bring us some comfort as we are grieving. When you step out of that pattern, it can be difficult, but can also lead to greater healing.

Never Say Goodbye

Those we love are never gone,
The bonds of love are much too strong,
Always only a thought away,
Within our hearts you will stay.

The physical body wasn't you,
Your eternal essence is what is true,
The earthly form has only changed,
Transitioning to heavenly gain.

One with God, and at peace,
Blessed the sweet release,
We can't help mourn for what we miss,
But we'll take comfort in knowing this.

Thank you for all our years of sharing,
The memories of love and caring,
Emotions are hard, and though we cry,
We never really say good-bye.

Our Journey

Each of us has a journey to make,
Individual trails to take,
But we don't always know,
Which path we should follow.

To some the road is crystal clear,
Others have no idea,
Should they turn left or right,
Uneasy, not knowing what's in sight?

Sometimes the path seems straight,
Then along comes Fate,
Suddenly there's a detour,
That you don't know if you can endure.

I want to be able to get back on track,
Overcoming emotions of profound lack,
Show me the signs that point the way,
So I won't be lost for all my days.

With the map for my soul,
I will travel towards my goal,
With an internal beacon directing me,
Shining a light for me to see.

Phoenix

Ever since your demise,
I see the world with different eyes,
The world I thought I knew,
Now has a different view.

Through this loss, pain and ache,
There is a different road to take,
I don't know where it will go,
But I am on it, this I know.

Heal my shattered, broken heart,
Help me find a fresh new start,
I long to have my spirit mend,
Let me feel the love you send.

Like the Phoenix, I want to fly,
Wings outstretched, flying high,
So that when I am gone,
The message is, love lives on.

Phoenix Rising

I have two choices,
To stay crippled from a killing blow,
Or fight for the strength I hope to know,
To rise up from the ashes and be happy again,
Or merely exist until my life ends.

Like the Phoenix I struggle to rise,
My son wants me to dry my eyes,
I will not allow his death to be in vain,
In his life and love so much was gained.

I love him more than my heart can hold,
My love pours and overflows,
It is in love that we reunite,
Just beyond earthly sight.

The Phoenix is a symbol of recovery to see,
Especially after great calamity,
Rising from destruction in plumage of scarlet and gold,
Once more magnificent to behold.

Fire destroys but also rebuilds,
From the depths to new heights to fulfill,
I want to heal like the Phoenix bird,
A beautiful immortal soul in this world.

Sacred Union

Germany and Austria were our destination,
When my husband and I went on vacation,
There were many churches we had the chance to view,
Such a privilege to be able to do.

Centuries old churches in baroque grandeur,
Magnificent paintings in wondrous splendor,
Gilded angels and saints in gold,
Awe-inspiring to behold.

Mary figures with expressions of peace,
Lovingly gazing outward to bring all relief,
One feels the presence of God and his hosts,
Christ, the Son, and the Holy Ghost.

I lit a candle in every church we went in,
And said a prayer for my son in Heaven,
Many silent tears I cried,
For our beloved son who died.

My son, you are in spirit infused with joy,
In Heaven with all of God's envoys,
A sacred union to look forward to,
When my life is over and I join you.

Save A Place For Me

Save a place for me in Heaven,
I am knocking at the door,
When the time comes for me to enter,
You're the one I'll be looking for.

I am climbing God's stairway,
Toward that heavenly glow,
Focused on forever,
There's so much I want to know.

In the garden of the Divine,
All will be revealed,
I open my heart in acceptance,
Praying daily to be healed.

No more tears in Heaven,
Only love and peace prevail,
All burdens will be lifted,
When we move beyond the veil.

I feel your love surround me,
In God's heavenly embrace,
With a team of caring angels,
Guiding me with grace.

I love you more than ever,
And miss you every day,
Save a place for me in Heaven,
I am on my way.

Serenity Bench

A prayer from St. Francis of Assisi,
Carved on a bench by our son's trees,
Inspirational words about wisdom and courage,
Accepting change and not being discouraged.

After our son died we placed the bench there,
Where I often say this Serenity Prayer,
Asking for all heavenly aid,
Surrendering to the plan that was laid.

I sit on the bench and I cry,
Missing my son and asking why,
Amidst the blooms on his apple trees,
Gifts he left for us all to see.

One day I hope to only smile,
With all memories of my child,
And any tears cried will be of joy,
For the years we had with our precious boy.

Shattered by Loss

Broken and bleeding at the foot of the cross,
Shattered by my loss,
Every day I pray and say,
Please, God, take this pain away.

The burden is much too heavy for me to bear,
Let me become more aware,
Of a world that I cannot clearly see,
Comforted by the touch of divinity.

I long for the brush of angels' wings,
To hear heavenly choirs that sing,
I want to feel God's love,
And know that I am taken care of.

The universe is vast, and I am small,
But I am part of it all,
Clear away my doubts and fears,
Build my faith in coming years.

Show me what my part is,
I want to more fully live,
To put together my broken pieces,
Assured that love never ceases.

Soul's Cry

My son's always with me, yet physically gone,
Lord, give me the strength to draw upon,
I cannot do this by myself,
Surround me with heavenly help.

Lead me to the well inside,
Knowing love is the guide,
Quench the thirst that leaves me dry,
Answer my soul's cry.

As I drink deeply from the cup,
Refresh my soul and fill it up,
And with the sacred water of life,
Remove all torment and earthly strife.

Sword Through the Heart

Mary was given a prophecy,
When Jesus was a baby,
Simeon told her in so many words,
Her heart would one day be pierced with a sword.

Mary pondered the words that he said,
Thoughts going around in her head,
But how could she ever imagine,
The crucifixion that would happen?

I identify with Mary and the sword through her heart,
My son died too, and I am torn apart,
The anguish of losing a beloved son,
Is beyond most people's comprehension.

When a child dies, while not Christ on the cross,
Every mother feels the same loss,
Christ and Mary understand what mothers feel,
And with divine love and compassion help us to heal.

I pray for God's mercy and grace,
So that I may have this sword replaced,
And in its stead my heart be filled,
With peace and love by Spirit instilled.

In September 2009 my husband and I visited dear friends who live in Germany. We toured many beautiful cities in southern Germany and also went to Salzburg, Austria. While we were in Salzburg we went in several magnificent churches and cathedrals, and saw the statue shown on the following page in one of them. It was overwhelming to see Mary and Jesus depicted this way. I stood there with tears running down my face, identifying so strongly with Mary as a mother who has also had my heart pierced by a sword. I wrote this poem after that incredibly emotional experience.

The Bigger Picture

If I live the average number of years,
Calculated while I am here,
I am already two-thirds through,
With what I came here to do.

It gives one pause upon reflection,
Because there's so much to question,
Has the life you've lived so far,
Positively defined who you are?

Have you fulfilled your hopes and dreams?
Are you happy with what you've done and seen?
Have you tried your very best,
So in contentment you may rest?

We must pray for God's love and light,
To help us to keep shining bright,
It's easy to become disillusioned,
And to live in a state of confusion.

When life doesn't go as you planned,
It's so hard to understand,
You realize there's so much we don't know,
And that we really have little control.

The picture is much bigger than we can see,
In the plan of eternity,
There is no timeframe for a soul,
Only one consistent goal.

That is to experience, learn and grow,
So that we eventually come to know,
The sacred breath of life,
That unites us all in Heaven's light.

The Fabric of Life

Everything in life changes, rearranges,
Nothing ever stays the same,
Some events are expected, but others shock,
Such as tragedy and loss.

Cycles and seasons,
There are cosmic reasons,
A pattern that is being designed,
To be beautifully completed in time.

Like a needle and thread,
Sewing a picture as we tread,
We create a tapestry,
An intricate design of artistry.

Colors and shades of all different hues,
Grays and blacks, yellows and blues,
What pattern will we create,
Upon our life's template?

Free will and choices, destiny and fate,
Concepts for us to contemplate,
As we stitch row by row,
The cloth begins to slowly grow.

Will our picture be complete,
When in Heaven we will meet?
I want no tears, knots or coils,
Anything that would spoil.

All my effort and the years,
That I worked on while I was here,
To be content that my work was done,
From the time it was first begun.

With Us in Spirit

Earth has no sorrow that Heaven cannot heal,
My soul longs for this to be real,
These are the words on a memorial fountain we bought,
And I meditate on them a lot.

The fountain is in our back yard,
Where you worked very hard,
Chopping down weeds,
And planting your trees.

Mowing the grass and digging holes,
For the plantings we wanted to grow,
You are everywhere that I gaze,
Remembrances of all that you gave.

A sanctuary of faith and love,
That you are such a part of,
A spiritual oasis that helps bring you near,
Because you are not physically here.

Who could imagine that you would be gone,
But your spirit is here and lives on,
As I sit on our lovely patio,
Watching the fountain water flow.

I think of the years we had together,
All of the moments we have to treasure,
Searching for inner peace,
With heavenly grace to heal and release.

HELPFUL RESOURCES

Books

Bridge Between Worlds (Extraordinary Experiences That Changed Lives), by Dan Millman and Doug Childers (H J Kramer, 2009; originally published as Divine Interventions, Daybreak Books, 1999)

Healing Grief (Reclaiming Life After Any Loss), by James Van Praagh (Dutton, 2000; New American Library, 2001)

Reaching Through the Veil to Heal (Death, Grief, & Communicating with Loved Ones in Spirit), by Linda Drake (Llewellyn Publications, 2006)

The Shack, by William P. Young (Windblown Media, 2007)

Signs from Above (Your Angels' Messages about Your Life Purpose, Relationships, Health, and More), by Doreen Virtue and Charles Virtue (Hay House, 2009)

Tear Soup, by Pat Schweibert and Chuck DeKlyen (Grief Watch, 1999)

Walking in the Garden of Souls, by George Anderson and Andrew Barone (G.P. Putnam's Sons, 2001; published in paperback by Berkley Books)

When God Gets Physical, by Carol Harris Barton (Outcome Publishing, 2009)
This book includes a chapter, "Feather," describing a sign I received from Graham through a dear friend.

Wherever You Go, There You Are (Mindfulness Meditation in Everyday Life), by Jon Kabat-Zinn (Hyperion, 1994; with new Afterword, 2005)

Helpful Resources

Music

Compact Disks

Ashley's Songbook, by Alan Pedersen, available at http://www. everashleymusic.com/links.html

I Dreamed A Dream, by Susan Boyle, available online and in stores

A Little Farther Down the Road, by Alan Pedersen, available at http:// www.everashleymusic.com/links.html

More Songs From the Journey, by Alan Pedersen, available at http:// www.everashleymusic.com/links.html

Sacred Arias, by Andrea Bocelli, available online and in stores

Songs

Note: These are all available online for individual download from sites such as http://www.amazon.com and from music services such as iTunes, as well as on compact disk (listed in parentheses); many are also available as videos on http://www.YouTube.com.

"Angel," by Sarah McLachlan, (on Surfacing and Closer – The Best of Sarah McLachlan)

"Because You Loved Me," by Céline Dion (on Falling Into You)

"Bridge Over Troubled Water," by Johnny Cash (on American IV: The Man Comes Around)

"Cryin' for Me (Wayman's Song)," by Toby Keith (on American Ride)

"Far Away," by Nickelback (on All the Right Reasons)

"Forever Young," by Rod Stewart (on The Definitive Rod Stewart)

"Gone Too Soon," by Michael Jackson (on <u>Dangerous</u>)

"Heaven," by Los Lonely Boys (on <u>Los Lonely Boys</u>)

"Home," by Daughtry (on <u>Daughtry</u>)

"I Believe," by Diamond Rio (on <u>Diamond Rio: 16 Biggest Hits</u>)

"I Hope You Dance," by Lee Ann Womack (on <u>I Hope You Dance</u>)

"If I Could Be Where You Are," by Enya (on <u>Amarantine</u>)

"Lean on Me," by Bill Withers (on <u>The Best of Bill Withers – Lean on Me</u>)

"Let It Be," by The Beatles (on <u>Let It Be</u>)

"The Man Comes Around," by Johnny Cash (on <u>American IV: The Man Comes Around</u>)

"My Heart Will Go On," by Céline Dion (on <u>Let's Talk About Love</u>)

"My Immortal," by Evanescence (on <u>Fallen</u>)

"One More Day," by Diamond Rio (on <u>Diamond Rio: 16 Biggest Hits</u>)

"Please Remember," by LeAnn Rimes (on <u>Coyote Ugly (Soundtrack)</u>)

"Please Remember Me," by Tim McGraw (on <u>Greatest Hits</u>)

"The Promise," by Tracy Chapman (on <u>New Beginning</u>)

"Save a Place for Me," by Matthew West (on <u>Something to Say</u>)

"Somewhere Over the Rainbow," by Israel Kamakawiwo'ole (on <u>Alone in IZ World</u>)

Helpful Resources

"Stand By Me," by Ben E. King (on Ben E. King: Anthology)

"To Where You Are," by Josh Groban (on Josh Groban)

"We'll Meet Again," by Johnny Cash (on American IV: The Man Comes Around)

"When I Get Where I'm Going," by Brad Paisley (on Time Well Wasted)

"When I Go Away," by Levon Helm (on Electric Dirt)

"Who You'd Be Today," by Kenny Chesney (on The Road and the Radio)

"Wild Horses," by Susan Boyle (on I Dreamed a Dream)

"Wind Beneath My Wings," by Bette Midler (on Experience the Divine: Greatest Hits)

"You've Got a Friend," by James Taylor (on James Taylor: Greatest Hits, Vol. 1)

Web Sites

Angels Across the USA – http://www.angelsacrosstheusa.com/

Bereaved Parents of the USA – http://www.bereavedparentsusa.org/

My blog, A Mother's Tears – http://amotherstears.blogspot.com/

The Compassionate Friends – http://www.compassionatefriends.org/home.aspx

Contact Talk Radio – http://www.contacttalkradio.com/

Hay House Radio – http://www.hayhouseradio.com/

Walking Your Own Journey

❦

Walking Your Own Journey